Collins

Collins
German
Words

HarperCollins Publishers
Westerhill Road
Bishopbriggs
Glasgow
G64 2QT
Great Britain

Second Edition 2007

Reprint 10 9 8 7 6 5 4 3 2 1 0

© HarperCollins Publishers 2006, 2007

ISBN-13 978-0-00-725279-X
ISBN-10 0-00-725279-4

Collins® and Bank of English® are
registered trademarks of
HarperCollins Publishers Limited

www.collins.co.uk

A catalogue record for this book is available
from the British Library

Typeset by Davidson's Prepress, Glasgow

Printed in Italy by Rotolito Lombarda S.p.A.

This book is set in Collins Fedra, a typeface
specially created for Collins dictionaries by
Peter Bil'ak

Acknowledgements
We would like to thank those authors and
publishers who kindly gave permission for
copyright material to be used in the Collins
Word Web. We would also like to thank
Times Newspapers Ltd for providing
valuable data.

PUBLISHING DIRECTOR
Lorna Knight

EDITORIAL DIRECTOR
Michela Clari

MANAGING EDITOR
Maree Airlie

PROJECT CO-ORDINATOR
Gaëlle Amiot-Cadey

CONTRIBUTOR
Horst Kopleck

BASED ON THE COLLINS GEM GERMAN
VITAL VOCAB BY
Barbara I. Christie
Màiri MacGinn
Horst Kopleck
Veronika Schnorr

William Collins' dream of knowledge for all began with the publication of his first book in 1819. A self-educated mill worker, he not only enriched millions of lives, but also founded a flourishing publishing house. Today, staying true to this spirit, Collins books are packed with inspiration, innovation, and practical expertise. They place you at the centre of a world of possibility and give you exactly what you need to explore it.

Language is the key to this exploration, and at the heart of Collins Dictionaries is language as it is really used. New words, phrases, and meanings spring up every day, and all of them are captured and analysed by the Collins Word Web. Constantly updated, and with over 2.5 billion entries, this living language resource is unique to our dictionaries.

Words are tools for life. And a Collins Dictionary makes them work for you.

Collins. Do more.

contents 5

6 contents

The *Easy Learning German Words* is designed for both young and adult learners. Whether you are starting to learn German for the very first time, revising for school exams or simply want to brush up on your German, the *Easy Learning German Words* offers you the information you require in a clear and accessible format.

This book is divided into 50 topics, arranged in alphabetical order. This thematic approach enables you to learn related words and phrases together, so that you can become confident in using particular vocabulary in context.

Vocabulary within each topic is divided into nouns and useful phrases which are aimed at helping you to express yourself in idiomatic German. Vocabulary within each topic is graded to help you prioritize your learning. Essential words include the basic words you will need to be able to communicate effectively, important words help expand your knowledge, and useful words provide additional vocabulary which will enable you to express yourself more fully.

Nouns are grouped by gender, which makes it easier to remember if they are masculine ("der") nouns, feminine ("die") nouns and neuter ("das") nouns. In addition, all plural forms are shown, with the exception of feminine nouns ending in –in (these regularly become –innen in the plural) and those forms, of whatever gender, which have the same form in both singular and plural.

Nouns which have been derived from adjectives follow the style:

Alte(r), -n   old man/woman

This means that the noun ending depends on whether the article is definite or indefinite, masculine or feminine, singular or plural. For example:

der Alte	*masculine singular (definite article)*
ein Alter	*masculine singular (indefinite article)*
die Alte	*feminine singular (definite article)*
eine Alte	*feminine singular (indefinite article)*
die Alten	*masculine and feminine singular (definite article)*
Alte	*masculine and feminine singular (no article)*

At the end of the book you will find a list of supplementary vocabulary, grouped according to part of speech – adjective, verb, noun and so on. This is vocabulary which you will come across in many everyday situations.

Finally, there is an English index which lists all the essential and important nouns given under the topic headings for quick reference.

The *Easy Learning German Words* helps you to consolidate your language learning. Together with the other titles in the *Easy Learning* range you can be sure that you have all the help you need when learning German at your fingertips.

ABBREVIATIONS

acc	accusative
adj	adjective
adv	adverb
conj	conjunction
dat	dative
etw	etwas (meaning *something*)
f	feminine
gen	genitive
jdm	jemandem (meaning *somebody – dative case*)
jdn	jemanden (meaning *somebody – accusative case*)
m	masculine
n	noun
nt	neuter
pl	plural
prep	preposition
sb	somebody
sth	something

ESSENTIAL WORDS (masculine)

der	Ausgang, ̈e	way out, exit
der	Ausstieg, -e	exit
der	Check-in, -s	check-in
der	Eingang, ̈e	entrance
der	Fahrgast, ̈e	passenger
der	Fahrkartenschalter	ticket office
der	Fahrplan, ̈e	timetable
die	Ferien (pl)	holiday
der	Flug, ̈e	flight
der	Fluggast, ̈e	airline passenger
der	Flughafen, ̈	airport
der	Flugplan, ̈e	flight schedule
der	Flugplatz, ̈e	airfield; airport
der	Flugpreis, -e	(air) fare
der	Flugschein, -e	(plane) ticket
der	Gepäckträger	porter
der	Gepäckwagen	luggage trolley
der	Geschäftsmann, -leute	businessman
der	Koffer	case, suitcase
der	Kofferkuli, -s	luggage trolley
der	Notausgang, ̈e	emergency exit
der	Pass, ̈e	passport
der	Passagier, -e	passenger
der	Personalausweis, -e	identity card
der	Reisende(r), -n	traveller
der	Reisepass, ̈e	passport
der	Sicherheitsbereich, -e	security area
der	Steward, -s	steward
der	Tourist, -en	tourist
der	Urlaub	holiday(s)
der	Urlauber	holidaymaker
der	Zoll	customs; duty
der	Zuschlag, ̈e	extra charge

air travel

ESSENTIAL WORDS (feminine)

die Ankunft, ¨e	arrival
die Auskunft, ¨e	information; information desk
die (einfache) Fahrkarte, -n	(single) ticket
die Gepäckausgabe	baggage reclaim
die Maschine, -n	plane
die Personenkontrolle, -n	checkpoint (for passengers)
die Reservierung, -en	booking, reservation
die Richtung, -en	direction
die Rückfahrkarte, -n	return (ticket)
die Sicherheitskontrolle, -n	security check
die Stewardess, -en	air hostess
die Tasche, -n	bag
die Toilette, -n	toilet
die Touristin	tourist
die Uhr, -en	clock; time
die Urlauberin	holiday-maker

ESSENTIAL WORDS (neuter)

das Fliegen	flying
das Flugzeug, -e	plane, aeroplane
das Fundbüro, -s	lost property office
das Gepäck	luggage
das Passagierflugzeug, -e	airliner
das Schließfach, ¨er	left luggage locker
das Taxi, -s	taxi
das Ticket, -s	(plane) ticket

USEFUL PHRASES

einen Flugschein or ein Ticket lösen to buy a (plane) ticket
einen Rückflug buchen to book a return flight
hin und zurück nach Köln a return to Cologne
ich packe I pack; ich packe aus I unpack
das Gepäck durchleuchten to scan the luggage
einchecken to check in; fliegen to fly; wir fliegen ab we fly off
erreichen to catch; verpassen to miss

IMPORTANT WORDS (masculine)

der	Abflug, ⏜e	takeoff, departure
der	Duty-free-Shop, -s	duty-free shop
der	Jumbojet, -s	jumbo jet
der	Kontrollturm, ⏜e	control tower
der	Metalldetektor, -en	metal detector
der	Pilot, -en	pilot
der	Sicherheitsbeamte(r), -n	security officer
der	Sicherheitsgurt, -e	seat belt
der	Start, -s	takeoff
der	Terminal, -s	(air) terminal
der	Terrorist, -en	terrorist
der	Zollbeamte(r), -n	customs officer

IMPORTANT WORDS (feminine)

die	Autovermietung, -en	car hire
die	Bordkarte, -n	boarding card
die	Landung, -en	landing
die	Sicherheitsbeamtin	security officer
die	Startbahn, -en	runway
die	Terroristin	terrorist
die	Verbindung, -en	connection
die	Verspätung, -en	delay
die	Zollkontrolle	customs control or check

IMPORTANT WORDS (neuter)

das	Abfluggate, -s	departure gate
das	E-Ticket, -s	e-ticket
das	Flugticket, -s	ticket
das	Handgepäck	hand luggage
das	Reisebüro, -s	travel agent's
das	Reiseziel, -e	destination

USEFUL PHRASES

starten to take off; beim Start during the takeoff
an Bord on board; luftkrank airsick
ein Flugzeug entführen to hijack a plane
landen to land; verspätet delayed, late

USEFUL WORDS (*masculine*)

der Anhänger	label, tag
der Aufkleber	sticker, label
der Babyraum, -̈e	mother and baby room
der Fluglotse, -n	air traffic controller
der Flugsteig, -e	gate

USEFUL WORDS (*feminine*)

die Besatzung, -en	crew
die Besucherterrasse, -n	spectator terrace
die Bombe, -n	bomb
die Gepäckermittlung	lost luggage office
die Landebahn, -en	runway
die Rollbahn, -en	runway
die Rolltreppe, -n	escalator
die Schallmauer	sound barrier
die Turbulenz	turbulence
die Wechselstube, -n	bureau de change
die Zwischenlandung, -en	stopover

USEFUL WORDS (*neuter*)

das Bodenpersonal	ground staff
das Durchleuchtungsgerät, -e	scanner
das Düsenflugzeug, -e	jet plane
das Restaurant, -s	restaurant

USEFUL PHRASES

einen Zuschlag zahlen to pay a supplement
zuschlagpflichtig subject to an extra charge
gültig valid
erhältlich available
durch den Zoll gehen to go through customs
verzollen to pay duty on
haben Sie etwas zu verzollen? do you have anything to declare?
nichts zu verzollen nothing to declare
zollfrei duty-free

ESSENTIAL WORDS (masculine)

der Elefant, -en	elephant
der Fisch, -e	fish
der Hals, ⸚e	neck; throat
der Hund, -e	dog
der Tiergarten, ⸚	zoo, zoological park
der Versuch, -e	experiment
der Zoo, -s	zoo

IMPORTANT WORDS (masculine)

der Affe, -n	monkey
der Bär, -en	bear
der Bock, ⸚e	buck, ram
der Hamster	hamster
der Huf, -e	hoof
der Löwe, -n	lion
der Schwanz, ⸚e	tail
der Tiger	tiger
der Wolf, ⸚e	wolf

ESSENTIAL WORDS (feminine)

die Katze, -n	cat
die Tierhandlung, -en	pet shop

IMPORTANT WORDS (feminine)

die Giraffe, -n	giraffe
die Hundehütte, -n	kennel
die Kuh, ⸚e	cow
die Löwin	lioness
die Maus, Mäuse	mouse
die Ratte, -n	rat
die Schlange, -n	snake
die Tigerin	tigress

USEFUL PHRASES

laufen to run; hüpfen to hop
springen to jump; kriechen to slither, crawl

ESSENTIAL WORDS (neuter)

das	Bein, -e	leg
das	Haar, -e	hair
das	Haustier, -e	pet
die	Jungen (pl)	young
das	Ohr, -en	ear
das	Tier, -e	animal

IMPORTANT WORDS (neuter)

das	Horn, ̈er	horn
das	Kamel, -e	camel
das	Känguru, -s	kangaroo
das	Kaninchen	rabbit
das	Krokodil, -e	crocodile
das	Pferd, -e	horse
das	Pony, -s	pony
das	Rhinozeros, -se	rhinoceros
das	Schaf, -e	sheep
das	Schwein, -e	pig
das	Zebra, -s	zebra

USEFUL PHRASES
wir haben keine Haustiere we don't have any pets
zahm tame; wild wild; gehorsam obedient
füttern to feed; fressen to eat
trinken to drink
schlafen to sleep
bellen to bark; miauen to miaow
knurren to growl; schnurren to purr
beißen to bite; kratzen to scratch
ich habe Angst vor Hunden I'm afraid of dogs

USEFUL WORDS *(masculine)*

der	Beutel	pouch *(of kangaroo)*
der	Bulle, -n	bull
der	Eisbär, -en	polar bear
der	Esel	donkey
der	Frosch, ⁻e	frog
der	Fuchs, ⁻e	fox
der	Hase, -n	hare
der	Hirsch, -e	stag
der	Höcker	hump *(of camel)*
der	Igel	hedgehog
der	Kater	tomcat
der	Maulwurf, ⁻e	mole
der	Ochse, -n	ox
der	Panzer	shell *(of tortoise)*
der	Pelz, -e	fur
der	Rüssel	snout *(of pig)*; trunk *(of elephant)*
der	Seehund, -e	seal
der	Stachel, -n	spine *(of hedgehog)*
der	Stier, -e	bull
der	Stoßzahn, ⁻e	tusk
der	Streifen	stripe *(of zebra)*
der	Wal(fisch), -e	whale
der	Ziegenbock, ⁻e	billy goat

USEFUL PHRASES
jagen to hunt; to shoot
zu Pferd on horseback
reiten gehen to go riding
auf die Fuchsjagd gehen to go fox-hunting
„Vorsicht, bissiger Hund" "beware of the dog"
der Hund wedelt mit dem Schwanz the dog wags its tail
die Katze streicheln to stroke the cat

USEFUL WORDS (feminine)

die	Falle, -n	trap
die	Fledermaus, -mäuse	bat
die	Heuschrecke, -n	grasshopper
die	Kralle, -n	claw; talon
die	Kröte, -n	toad
die	Mähne, -n	mane
die	Natter, -n	adder
die	Pfote, -n	paw (small)
die	Pranke, -n	paw (large)
die	Ringelnatter, -n	grass snake
die	Robbe, -n	seal
die	Schildkröte, -n	tortoise
die	Schnauze, -n	snout, muzzle
die	Tatze, -n	paw
die	Ziege, -n	goat, nanny goat

USEFUL WORDS (neuter)

das	Eichhörnchen	squirrel
das	Fell, -e	coat, fur
das	Geweih	antlers (pl)
das	Hufeisen	horseshoe
das	Maul, Mäuler	mouth
das	Maultier, -e	mule
das	Meerschweinchen	guinea pig
das	Merkmal, -e	characteristic
das	Nashorn, -er	rhinoceros
das	Nilpferd, -e	hippopotamus
das	Reh, -e	roe deer

USEFUL PHRASES

ein Tier freilassen to set an animal free
ein Löwe ist aus dem Zoo entlaufen a lion has escaped from the zoo
in eine Falle gehen to be caught in a trap

ESSENTIAL + IMPORTANT WORDS *(masculine)*

der	Gang, ⸚e	gear
der	Gepäckträger	luggage carrier
der	Motorradfahrer	motorcyclist
der	Radfahrer	cyclist
der	Rad(fahr)weg, -e	cycle track *or* path
der	Radsport	cycling
der	Reifen	tyre
der	Sattel, ⸚	saddle, seat

ESSENTIAL + IMPORTANT WORDS *(feminine)*

die	Achtung	attention
die	Bahn, -en	road, way; (cycle) lane
die	Bremse, -n	brake
die	Ecke, -n	corner
die	Fahrradlampe, -n	cycle lamp
die	Gefahr, -en	danger, risk
die	Geschwindigkeit, -en	speed
die	Hauptstraße, -n	main street, main road
die	Kette, -n	chain
die	Klingel, -n	bell
die	Lampe, -n	lamp
die	Nebenstraße, -n	side street
die	Pumpe, -n	pump
die	Radfahrerin	cyclist
die	Reifenpanne, -n	puncture
die	Reparatur, -en	repair; repairing

USEFUL PHRASES

mit dem (Fahr)rad fahren to cycle
mit dem Rad in die Stadt fahren to cycle into town
er kam mit dem Rad he came on his bike, he came by bike
„Radfahren verboten" "cycling prohibited"
Radsport betreiben to go in for cycling
aufsteigen to get on; absteigen to get off
bergauf uphill; bergab downhill
klingeln to ring one's bell; schalten to change gear

ESSENTIAL WORDS (neuter)

das Fahrrad, ⁻er	bicycle
das Hinterrad, ⁻er	back wheel
das Motorrad, ⁻er	motorbike, motorcycle
das Pedal, -e	pedal
das Rad, ⁻er	wheel; bike
das Radfahren	cycling
das Vorderrad, ⁻er	front wheel

USEFUL WORDS (masculine)

der Dynamo, -s	dynamo
der Helm, -e	helmet
der Korb, ⁻e	pannier; basket
der Rückstrahler	reflector

USEFUL WORDS (feminine)

die Lenkstange, -n	handlebars
die Satteltasche, -n	saddlebag, pannier
die Speiche, -n	spoke
die Steigung, -en	gradient
die Straßenverkehrsordnung	Highway Code

USEFUL WORDS (neuter)

das Flickzeug, -e	puncture repair kit
das Katzenauge, -n	rear light; reflector; cat's eye
das Moped, -s	moped
das Mountainbike, -s	mountain bike
das Schutzblech, -e	mudguard

USEFUL PHRASES

bremsen to brake; reparieren to repair
einen Platten haben to have a flat tyre
geplatzt burst; kaputt broken, done
das Loch flicken to mend the puncture
die Reifen aufpumpen to blow up the tyres
glänzend shiny; rostig rusty; Leucht- fluorescent

ESSENTIAL + IMPORTANT WORDS (masculine)

der	Flamingo, -s	flamingo
der	Hahn, ⁝e	cock
der	Himmel	sky
der	Käfig, -e	cage
der	Kanarienvogel, ⁝	canary
der	Kuckuck, -e	cuckoo
der	Pinguin, -e	penguin
der	Schwan, ⁝e	swan
der	Storch, ⁝e	stork
der	Truthahn, ⁝e	turkey
der	Vogel, ⁝	bird
der	Wellensittich, -e	budgie, budgerigar

ESSENTIAL + IMPORTANT WORDS (feminine)

die	Ente, -n	duck
die	Feder, -n	feather
die	Gans, ⁝e	goose
die	Henne, -n	hen
die	Luft	air
die	Nachtigall, -en	nightingale

ESSENTIAL + IMPORTANT WORDS (neuter)

das	Huhn, ⁝er	hen, fowl
das	Nest, -er	nest
das	Rotkehlchen	robin (redbreast)
das	or der (Vogel)bauer	birdcage

USEFUL PHRASES

fliegen to fly; abfliegen to fly away
ein Nest bauen to build a nest; nisten to nest
Eier legen to lay eggs
singen to sing
pfeifen to whistle
zwitschern to twitter
Lärm machen to make a noise

USEFUL WORDS (masculine)

der Adler	eagle
der Eisvogel, ¨	kingfisher
der Falke, -n	falcon
der Fasan, -e(n)	pheasant
der Fink, -en	finch
der Flügel	wing
der Geier	vulture
der Habicht, -e	hawk
der Hirtenstar, -s	mynah bird
der Papagei, -en	parrot
der Pfau, -en	peacock
der Puter	turkey(-cock)
der Rabe, -n	raven
der Schnabel, ¨	beak, bill
der Sittich, -e	parakeet
der Spatz, -en	sparrow
der Specht, -e	woodpecker
der Sperling, -e	sparrow
der Star, -e	starling
der Strauß, -e	ostrich
der Zaunkönig, -e	wren

USEFUL WORDS (feminine)

die Amsel, -n	blackbird
die Blaumeise, -n	bluetit
die Dohle, -n	jackdaw
die Drossel, -n	thrush
die Elster, -n	magpie
die Eule, -n	owl
die Krähe, -n	crow
die Lerche, -n	lark
die Möwe, -n	seagull
die Saatkrähe, -n	rook
die Schwalbe, -n	swallow
die Taube, -n	dove; pigeon

ESSENTIAL WORDS (*masculine*)

der	**Arm, -e**	arm
der	**Bauch, Bäuche**	stomach
der	**Finger**	finger
der	**Fuß, ̈e**	foot
der	**Hals, ̈e**	neck, throat
der	**Kopf, ̈e**	head
der	**Magen, - or ̈**	stomach
der	**Mund, ̈er**	mouth
der	**Rücken**	back
der	**Zahn, ̈e**	tooth

ESSENTIAL WORDS (*feminine*)

die	**Bewegung, -en**	movement, motion
die	**Hand, ̈e**	hand
die	**Nase, -n**	nose
die	**Seite, -n**	side

ESSENTIAL WORDS (*neuter*)

das	**Auge, -n**	eye
das	**Bein, -e**	leg
das	**Fleisch**	flesh
das	**Gesicht, -er**	face
das	**Haar, -e**	hair
das	**Ohr, -en**	ear

USEFUL PHRASES

ich habe mir den Arm/das Bein gebrochen I've broken my arm/leg
mein Arm/Bein tut weh my arm/leg hurts
zu Fuß on foot; barfuß gehen to go *or* walk barefoot
von Kopf bis Fuß from head to foot, from top to toe
den Kopf schütteln to shake one's head
mit den Kopf nicken to nod one's head
jdm die Hand geben to shake hands with sb
(mit der Hand) winken to wave
auf etwas zeigen to point to something

IMPORTANT WORDS (masculine)

der	Atem	breath
der	Daumen	thumb
der	Körper	body
der	Körperteil, -e	part of the body
der	Zeigefinger	forefinger, index finger

IMPORTANT WORDS (feminine)

die	Lippe, -n	lip
die	Schulter, -n	shoulder
die	Stimme, -n	voice
die	Zunge, -n	tongue

IMPORTANT WORDS (neuter)

das	Blut	blood
das	Herz, -en	heart
das	Knie	knee

USEFUL PHRASES

sehen to see; hören to hear
fühlen to feel; riechen to smell
tasten to touch; schmecken to taste
sich die Nase putzen to blow one's nose
jdm auf die Schulter klopfen to tap sb on the shoulder
sein Herz klopfte his heart was beating
die linke/rechte Körperseite the left-hand/right-hand side of the body
neben mir at my side
eine leise/laute Stimme haben to have a soft/loud voice
leise/laut sprechen to speak softly/loudly
ich lasse mir die Haare schneiden I'm having my hair cut
auf den Knien on one's knees
stehen to stand; sitzen to sit
sich legen to lie down; knien to kneel (down)
bewegen to move (part of the body)
sich bewegen to move

USEFUL WORDS *(masculine)*

der	Ell(en)bogen	elbow
der	(Fuß)knöchel	ankle
der	Hintern	bottom
der	Kiefer	jaw
der	Knöchel	knuckle; ankle
der	Knochen	bone
der	Muskel, -n	muscle
der	Nacken	nape of the neck
der	Nagel, ∺	nail
der	Nerv, -en	nerve
der	Schenkel	thigh

USEFUL WORDS *(neuter)*

das	(Augen)lid, -er	eyelid
das	Blutgefäß, -e	blood vessel
das	Fußgelenk, -e	ankle
das	Gehirn, -e	brain
das	Gelenk, -e	joint
das	Genick, -e	nape of the neck
das	Glied, -er	limb
das	Handgelenk, -e	wrist
das	Kinn, -e	chin
die	Maße *(pl)*	measurements
das	Rückgrat, -e	spine
das	Skelett, -e	skeleton

USEFUL PHRASES

ich habe mir den Knöchel verstaucht I've sprained my ankle
biegen to bend; strecken to stretch
stürzen to fall; verletzen, verwunden to injure
müde tired
fit fit; unfit unfit
ich ruhe mich aus I'm resting *or* having a rest
taub deaf; blind blind; stumm dumb
körperbehindert physically handicapped
geistig behindert mentally handicapped

USEFUL WORDS *(feminine)*

die	Ader, -n	vein
die	Arterie, -n	artery
die	Augenbraue, -n	eyebrow
die	(Augen)wimper, -n	eyelash
die	Brust, ¨e	breast; chest
die	Faust, Fäuste	fist
die	Ferse, -n	heel
die	Figur, -en	figure
die	Form, -en	shape, figure
die	Fußsohle, -n	sole of the foot
die	Gestalt, -en	figure, form, shape
die	Geste, -n	gesture
die	Haut	skin
die	Hüfte, -n	hip
die	Kehle, -n	throat
die	Leber, -n	liver
die	Lunge, -n	lung
die	Niere, -n	kidney
die	Pupille, -n	pupil (*of eye*)
die	Rippe, -n	rib
die	Schläfe, -n	temple
die	Schlagader, -n	artery
die	Stirn, -en	forehead
die	Taille, -n	waist
die	Wade, -n	calf (*of leg*)
die	Wange, -n	neck
die	Zehe, -n	toe
die	große Zehe, -n -n	big toe

USEFUL PHRASES

Brustumfang *(m)* bust or chest measurement
Hüftweite *(f)* hip measurement
Taillenweite *(f)* waist measurement

THE SEASONS

der **Frühling**	spring
der **Sommer**	summer
der **Herbst**	autumn
der **Winter**	winter

im Frühling/Sommer/Herbst/Winter in spring/summer/autumn/winter

THE MONTHS

Januar	January	**Juli**	July
Februar	February	**August**	August
März	March	**September**	September
April	April	**Oktober**	October
Mai	May	**November**	November
Juni	June	**Dezember**	December

im September *etc* in September *etc*
der erste April April Fools' Day
der Erste Mai May Day
der fünfte November (*Tag der Pulververschwörung in England*) Guy Fawkes
Night

THE DAYS OF THE WEEK

Montag	Monday
Dienstag	Tuesday
Mittwoch	Wednesday
Donnerstag	Thursday
Freitag	Friday
Samstag } **Sonnabend** }	Saturday
Sonntag	Sunday

USEFUL PHRASES

freitags *etc* on Fridays *etc*
am Freitag *etc* on Friday *etc*
nächsten/letzten Freitag *etc* next/last Friday *etc*
am nächsten Freitag *etc* the following Friday *etc*

THE CALENDAR

Advent (*m*) Advent
der Adventskranz Advent wreath
Allerheiligen (*nt*) All Saints' Day
der Abend vor Allerheiligen Hallowe'en
Allerseelen (*nt*) All Souls' Day
Aschermittwoch (*m*) Ash Wednesday
Dreikönigfest (*nt*) Epiphany, Twelfth Night
Faschingszeit (*f*) the Fasching festival, carnival time
Fastenzeit (*f*) Lent
Fastnacht (*f*) Shrove Tuesday
Heiliger Abend, Heiligabend (*m*) Christmas Eve
Karfreitag (*m*) Good Friday
Neujahr (*nt*) New Year
Neujahrstag (*m*) New Year's Day
Ostern (*nt*) Easter
Ostersonntag (*m*) Easter Sunday
Palmsonntag (*m*) Palm Sunday
Passahfest (*nt*) (Feast of the) Passover
Pfingsten (*nt*) Whitsun
Pfingstmontag (*m*) Whit Monday
Silvester (*nt*) New Year's Eve, Hogmanay
Silvesterabend (*m*) New Year's Eve, Hogmanay
Valentinstag (*m*) St Valentine's Day
der Valentinsgruß Valentine card
Weihnachten (*nt*) Christmas
Weihnachtsabend (*m*) Christmas Eve
Weihnachtstag (*m*) Christmas Day
zweiter Weihnachtstag (*m*) Boxing Day
die Weihnachtskarte Christmas card

USEFUL PHRASES

zu Weihnachten/Ostern/Pfingsten at Christmas/Easter/Whitsun

SPECIAL EVENTS

die	**Beerdigung, -en**	funeral, burial
die	**Bescherung, -en**	distribution of Christmas presents
der	**Feiertag, -e**	holiday
das	**Festival, -s**	festival
der	**Festtag, -e**	holiday
das	**Feuerwerk, -e**	firework display
der	**Feuerwerkskörper**	firework
der	**Friedhof, ⁻e**	cemetery, graveyard
der	**Geburstag, -e**	birthday
das	**Geschenk, -e**	present
die	**Heirat, -en**	marriage
der	**Hochzeitstag, -e**	wedding day
die	**Jahreszeit, -en**	season
der	**Kalender**	calendar
das	**Konfetti**	confetti
der	**Wochentag, -e**	weekday
der	**Tanz, ⁻e** *or* **Tanzabend**	dance
die	**Taufe, -n**	christening, baptism
der	**Tod, -e**	death
der	**Werktag, -e**	working day
der	**Zirkus, -se**	circus

USEFUL PHRASES

seinen Geburtstag feiern to celebrate one's birthday
der Silvestertanz New Year's Eve dance
prosit Neujahr! happy New Year!
jdm ein Geschenk machen to give somebody a present
ein Feuerwerk abbrennen to set off fireworks
ihr dritter Hochzeitstag their third (wedding) anniversary
beglückwünschen (zu) to congratulate (on)
wünschen to wish
(herzlich) willkommen! you are (very) welcome!
in Trauer in mourning
den Wievielten haben wir heute? what is today's date?

SPECIAL EVENTS

die	Blaskapelle, -n	brass band
das	Fest, -e	fête, feast (day)
die	Flitterwochen (pl)	honeymoon (time)
das	Folksongfestival	folk music festival
die	Geburt, -en	birth
die	Hochzeit, -en	wedding
die	Hochzeitsreise, -n	honeymoon (journey)
der	Jahrmarkt, ¨e	fair
die	Kirchweih, -en	fair
die	Kirmes, -sen	funfair
die	Messe, -n	(commercial) fair
der	Namenstag, -e	saint's day
die	Party, -s	party
der	Ruhestand	retirement
der	Rummelplatz, ¨e	fairground
die	Trauung, -en	wedding ceremony
die	Verabredung, -en	date (with sb)
die	Verlobung, -en	engagement
das	Volksfest	funfair
die	Zeremonie, -n	ceremony

USEFUL PHRASES

auf eine or zu einer Hochzeit gehen to go to a wedding
silberne/goldene/diamantene Hochzeit silver/golden/diamond wedding
in den Ruhestand gehen to retire, go into retirement
die Stadt mit Blumen ausschmücken to decorate the town with flowers
die ganze Stadt war beflaggt there were flags out all over town
gute Vorsätze fassen to make good resolutions
beerdigen to bury

ESSENTIAL WORDS *(masculine)*

der	**Camper**	camper *(person)*
der	**Campingplatz, ⁀e**	camp site
der	**Löffel**	spoon
der	**Rucksack, ⁀e**	backpack, rucksack
der	**Schlafsack, ⁀e**	sleeping bag
der	**Teller**	plate
der	**Urlaub**	holiday(s)
der	**Wohnwagen**	caravan
der	**Zuschlag, ⁀e**	extra charge

ESSENTIAL WORDS *(feminine)*

die	**Anmeldung, -en**	registration
die	**Camperin**	camper *(person)*
die	**Dusche, -n**	shower
die	**Gabel, -n**	fork
die	**Landkarte, -n**	map
die	**Luft, ⁀e**	air
die	**Nacht, ⁀e**	night
die	**Sache, -n**	thing
die	**Tasse, -n**	cup
die	**Toilette, -n**	toilet
die	**Übernachtung, -en**	overnight stay
die	**Waschmaschine, -n**	washing machine

ESSENTIAL WORDS *(neuter)*

das	**Camping**	camping
das	**Essen**	food; meal
das	**Glas, ⁀er**	glass
das	**Messer**	knife
das	**(Trink)wasser**	(drinking) water
das	**Zelt, -e**	tent

USEFUL PHRASES

Camping machen to go camping
ein Zelt aufbauen *or* aufschlagen to pitch a tent
ein Zelt abbauen to take down a tent
„Zelten verboten!" "no camping"

IMPORTANT + USEFUL WORDS *(masculine)*

der	Aufenthalt, -e	stay
der	Campingkocher	camping stove
der	Dosenöffner	tin-opener
der	Feuerlöscher	fire extinguisher
der	Klappstuhl, ˙-e	folding chair
der	Klapptisch, -e	folding table
der	Korkenzieher	corkscrew
der	Liegestuhl, ˙-e	deck chair
der	Mülleimer	dustbin
der	Rasierapparat, -e	razor
der	Schatten	shade; shadow
der	Waschraum, -räume	washroom
der	Zeltboden, ˙-	ground sheet
der	Zimmernachweis, -e	accommodation office

IMPORTANT + USEFUL WORDS *(feminine)*

die	Büchse, -n	tin, can; box
die	Luftmatratze, -n	lilo, air bed
die	Nachtruhe	lights-out
die	Ruhe	peace; rest
die	Taschenlampe, -n	torch
die	Unterkunft, ˙-e	accommodation
die	Veranstaltung, -en	organization
die	Wäsche	washing (things)
die	Wäscherei, -en	laundry (place)

IMPORTANT + USEFUL WORDS *(neuter)*

das	Campinggas	camping gas
das	Fahrzeug, -e	vehicle
das	Geschirr	dishes, crockery; pots and pans
das	Lagerfeuer	campfire
das	Streichholz, ˙-er	match
das	Waschpulver	washing powder, detergent
das	Wohnmobil, -e	camper, motor caravan

ESSENTIAL WORDS (*masculine*)

der	Arbeiter	worker, labourer
	Arbeitslose(r), -n	unemployed man/woman
der	Arzt, ⁻e	doctor
der	Briefträger	postman
der	Chef, -s	boss, head
der	Geschäftsmann, -leute	businessman
der	Job, -s	(spare time) job
der	Koch, ⁻e	cook
der	Krankenpfleger	nurse
der	Last(kraft)wagenfahrer;	lorry driver
	der Lkw-Fahrer	
der	Lehrer	teacher
der	Polizist, -en	policeman
der	Taxifahrer	taxi driver
der	Techniker	technician
der	Teilzeitjob, -s	part-time job
der	Zahnarzt, ⁻e	dentist

ESSENTIAL WORDS (*feminine*)

die	Arbeit, -en	work; job
die	Arbeiterin	worker
die	Ärztin	doctor
die	Bank, -en	bank
die	Bezahlung, -en	payment
die	Chefin	boss
die	Empfangsdame, -n	receptionist
die	Fabrik, -en	factory
die	Geschäftsfrau, -en	businesswoman
die	Geschäftsreise, -n	business trip
die	Industrie, -n	industry
die	Köchin	cook
die	Krankenschwester, -n	nurse
die	Lehrerin	teacher
die	Polizistin	policewoman
die	Zahnärztin	dentist

ESSENTIAL WORDS *(neuter)*

das	**Büro, -s**	office
das	**Geschäft, -e**	business, trade; shop
das	**Jobcenter, -s**	job centre

USEFUL PHRASES

arbeiten to work; bei X arbeiten to work at X's
interessant interesting; langweilig boring
mit der Arbeit anfangen, zu arbeiten beginnen to start work,
   get down to work
berufstätig sein to be employed
arbeitslos sein to be out of work, be unemployed
arbeitslos werden to be made redundant
Arbeitslosengeld beziehen to be on the dole
seine Stelle verlieren to lose one's job
entlassen to dismiss
entlassen werden to be sacked, get the sack
jobben to do odd jobs
eine Stelle suchen to look for a job
„Stellenangebote" "situations vacant"
fest permanent; vorübergehend temporary
ganztags full-time; halbtags part-time
sich um eine Stelle bewerben to apply for a job
eine Stelle antreten to start a new job
verdienen to earn
500 Pfund in der Woche verdienen to earn £500 per week
sparen für (+ *acc*) to save up for
was sind Sie von Beruf? what is your job?
ich bin Elektriker (von Beruf) I am an electrician (to trade)
ehrgeizig ambitious
selbstständig self-employed
ich möchte Sekretärin werden I'd like to be a secretary
sein eigenes Geschäft haben to have one's own shop or business
eine Geschäftsreise machen to go away on business
streiken to strike, be on strike

IMPORTANT WORDS (*masculine*)

	Angestellte(r), -n	employee
der	Apotheker	chemist
der	Arbeitgeber	employer
der	Arbeitslohn, ⁻e	wages, pay
der	Arbeitnehmer	employee
der	Architekt, -en	architect
der	Arzthelfer	doctor's receptionist
der	Astronaut, -en	astronaut
der	Bankkaufmann, -leute	bank clerk
der	Bäcker	baker
	Beamte(r), -n	official
der	Beruf, -e	profession, occupation
der	Betrieb, -e	firm, concern
der	Bibliothekar, -e	librarian
	Büroangestellte(r), -n	office worker, clerk
der	Elektriker	electrician
der	Feuerwehrmann, -männer	fireman
der	Fotograf, -en	photographer
der	Friseur, -e	hairdresser
der	Geschäftsführer	executive; manager
der	Informatiker	computer scientist
der	Ingenieur, -e	engineer
der	Journalist, -en	journalist
der	Kfz-Mechaniker	motor mechanic
der	Lehrling, -e	apprentice, trainee
der	Lohn, ⁻e	wages, pay
der	Maler	painter
der	Pilot, -en	pilot
der	Politiker	politician
der	Präsident, -en	president
der	Premierminister	prime minister, premier
der	Priester	priest
der	Reporter	reporter
der	Sekretär, -e	secretary
der	Star, -s	star
der	Tierarzt, ⁻e	veterinary surgeon, vet
der	Verkäufer	salesman, shop assistant
der	Webdesigner	Web designer

IMPORTANT WORDS *(feminine)*

die	Arbeitnehmerin	employee
die	Architektin	architect
die	Arzthelferin	doctor's receptionist
die	Astronautin	astronaut
die	Bäckerin	baker
die	Bankkauffrau, -en	bank clerk
die	Beamtin	official
die	Berufsberatung	careers or vocational guidance
die	Bewerbung	application
die	Bibliothekarin	librarian
die	Firma, Firmen	firm, company
die	Friseuse, -n	hairdresser
die	Geschäftsführerin	executive; manageress
die	Gesellschaft, -en	company
die	Informatikerin	computer scientist
die	Journalistin	journalist
die	Kfz-Mechanikerin	motor mechanic
die	Lehrzeit, -en	apprenticeship
die	Politikerin	politician
die	Putzfrau, -en	cleaner, cleaning woman
die	Sekretärin	secretary
die	Stelle, -n	job, post
die	Tagesmutter, ⁻	child minder
die	Tierärztin	veterinary surgeon, vet
die	Verkäuferin	salesgirl, shop assistant
die	Webdesignerin	Web designer
die	Zukunft	future

IMPORTANT WORDS *(neuter)*

das	Einkommen	income
das	Gehalt, ⁻er	salary
das	Handwerk, -e	trade; craft
das	Kindermädchen	nanny
das	Model, -s	model

USEFUL WORDS *(masculine)*

	Abgeordnete(r), -n	M.P., member of parliament
der	Augenoptiker	optician
der	Autor, -en	author
der	Bauunternehmer	builder, building contractor
der	Bergarbeiter	miner
der	Betriebsleiter	managing director
der	Chirurg, -en	surgeon
der	Dichter	poet
der	Dolmetscher	interpreter
der	Florist, -en	florist
der	Forscher	researcher
der	Gewerkschaftler	trade unionist
der	Handel	commerce
der	Hausmeister	caretaker; janitor
der	Hotelfachmann, -leute	hotel manager
der	Kameramann, -männer	cameraman
der	Klempner	plumber
der	König, -e	king
der	Künstler	artist
der	Matrose, -n	sailor
der	Modeschöpfer	fashion designer
der	Mönch, -e	monk
der	Pfarrer	minister, clergyman
der	Produzent, -en	manufacturer; (film) producer
der	Rechtsanwalt, ̈e	lawyer, solicitor
der	Redakteur, -e	editor
der	Schneider	tailor
der	Schriftsteller	writer
der	Soldat, -en	soldier
der	Tischler	joiner, carpenter
der	Verleger	publisher
der	Vertreter	representative, rep
	Vorsitzende(r), -n	chairman/-woman
der	Winzer	wine grower, vineyard owner
der	Wirtschaftsprüfer	chartered accountant
der	Wissenschaftler	scientist

USEFUL WORDS *(feminine)*

die	**Absicht, -en**	intention, aim
die	**Augenoptikerin**	optician
die	**Ausbildung**	training, education
die	**Autorin**	author
die	**Chirurgin**	surgeon
die	**Dichterin**	poet
die	**Dolmetscherin**	interpreter
die	**Floristin**	florist
die	**Forscherin**	researcher
die	**Gewerkschaft, -en**	trade union
die	**Hotelfachfrau, -en**	hotel manageress
die	**Jobvermittlung, -en**	employment agency
die	**Kamerafrau, -en**	camerawoman
die	**Königin**	queen
die	**Künstlerin**	artist
die	**Laufbahn, -en**	career
die	**Leiterin**	leader, manager
die	**Lohnerhöhung, -en**	wage increase
die	**Modeschöpferin**	fashion designer
die	**Nonne, -n**	nun
die	**Platzanweiserin**	usherette
die	**Rechtsanwältin**	lawyer, solicitor
die	**Redakteurin**	editor
die	**Schneiderin**	dressmaker
die	**Schriftstellerin**	writer
die	**Soldatin**	soldier
die	**Sprechstundenhilfe, -n**	(medical) receptionist
die	**Stenotypistin**	shorthand typist
die	**Stewardess, -en**	flight attendant
die	**Verwaltung, -en**	administration
die	**Wissenschaftlerin**	scientist

ESSENTIAL WORDS (masculine)

der	(Auto)fahrer	motorist, driver
der	Diesel	diesel (oil)
der	Führerschein, -e	driving licence
der	Kilometer	kilometre
der	Koffer	suitcase
der	Lastkraftwagen (Lkw)	lorry, truck
der	Lastwagenfahrer	lorry driver
der	Liter	litre
der	Parkplatz, ⸚e	parking space; car park
der	Passagier, -e	passenger
der	Personenkraftwagen (Pkw)	private car
der	Polizist, -en	policeman
der	Rasthof, ⸚e	service station
der	Rastplatz, ⸚e	lay-by
der	Reifen	tyre
der	Reifendruck	tyre pressure
der	(Sport)wagen	(sports) car
der	Weg, -e	road, way
der	Wohnwagen	caravan

ESSENTIAL WORDS (neuter)

das	Auto, -s	car
das	Benzin, -e	petrol
das	Dieselöl	diesel (oil)
das	Gepäck	luggage
das	Mietauto, -s	hired car
das	Normalbenzin	2-star (petrol)
das	Öl, -e	oil
das	Parkhaus, -häuser	(covered) multistorey car park
das	Parken	parking
das	Rad, ⸚er	wheel
das	Selbsttanken	self-service petrol
das	Straßenschild, -er	road sign
das	Super	4-star (petrol)
das	Wasser	water

ESSENTIAL WORDS *(feminine)*

die	Achtung	attention
die	Ampel, -n	traffic lights
die	Ausfahrt, -en	exit; drive; slip road
die	Autobahn, -en	motorway
die	(Auto)fahrerin	motorist, driver
die	Bahn, -en	road, way; lane
die	Batterie, -n	battery
die	Ecke, -n	corner
die	Einbahnstraße, -n	one-way street
die	Fahrt, -en	journey; trip; drive
die	Garage, -n	garage
die	Hauptstraße, -n	main road, main street
die	grüne Versicherungskarte, -n, -n	green card
die	Landkarte, -n	map
die	Maschine, -n	engine
die	Meile, -n	mile
die	Polizei	police
die	Polizistin	policewoman
die	Raststätte, -n	service area
die	Reise, -n	journey
die	Reparatur, -en	repair; repairing
die	(Reparatur)werkstatt, ¨en	garage, workshop
die	Richtung, -en	direction
die	Selbstbedienung (SB)	self-service
die	Straße, -n	street, road
die	Straßenkarte, -n	road map, plan
die	Straßenverkehrsordnung	Highway Code
die	Tankstelle, -n	petrol station, filling station, service station
die	Umleitung, -en	diversion
die	Verkehrsampel, -n	traffic lights
die	Vorfahrt	right of way
die	Vorsicht	caution, care
die	Warnung, -en	warning
die	Werkstatt, ¨en	garage, workshop

IMPORTANT WORDS (masculine)

der	Abstand, ⸚e	distance
der	Blinker	indicator
der	Chauffeur, -e	chauffeur
der	Dachgepäckträger	roof rack
der	Fahrlehrer	driving instructor
der	Fahrschüler	learner driver
der	Fußgänger	pedestrian
der	Gang, ⸚e	gear
der	Kofferraum, -räume	boot
der	Mechaniker	mechanic; engineer
der	Motorschaden, -schäden	engine trouble
der	Parkschein, -e	parking permit
der	Rückspiegel	rear-view or driving mirror
der	Scheinwerfer	headlight, headlamp
der	Sicherheitsgurt, -e	seat belt
der	Stau, -e	(traffic) jam
der	Tramper	hitch-hiker
der	Umweg, -e	detour
der	Unfall, ⸚e	accident
der	Verkehr	traffic
der	Verkehrspolizist, -en	traffic warden
der	Verkehrsunfall, ⸚e	road accident
	Verletzte(r), -n	casualty
der	Zusammenstoß, ⸚e	collision, crash

IMPORTANT WORDS (neuter)

das	Autobahndreieck, -e	motorway junction
das	Autobahnkreuz, -e	motorway intersection
das	Fahrzeug, -e	vehicle
das	Firmenauto, -s	company car
das	Navigationssystem, -e	(satellite) navigation system
das	Parkverbot, -e	parking ban
das	Reserverad, ⸚er	spare wheel
das	Trampen	hitch-hiking
das	Wohngebiet, -e	built-up area

IMPORTANT WORDS *(feminine)*

die	Autoschlange, -n	line of cars
die	Autowäsche, -n	car wash
die	Bremse, -n	brake
die	Fahrlehrerin	driving instructress
die	Fahrprüfung, -en	driving test
die	Fahrschule, -n	driving school
die	Fahrschülerin	learner driver
die	Fahrstunde, -n	driving lesson
die	Gebühr, -en	toll
die	Gefahr, -en	danger, risk
die	Geldstrafe, -n	fine
die	Geschwindigkeit, -en	speed
die	Grenze, -n	border, frontier
die	Hauptverkehrszeit, -en	rush hour
die	Kreuzung, -en	crossroads
die	Kurve, -n	bend, corner
die	Notbremsung, -en	emergency stop
die	Panne, -n	breakdown
die	Parkuhr, -en	parking meter
die	Querstraße, -n	junction, intersection
die	Reifenpanne, -n	puncture
die	(Reise)route, -n	route, itinerary
die	Ringstraße, -n	ring road
die	Tiefgarage, -n	underground garage
die	Verkehrspolizistin	traffic warden
die	Versicherung, -en	insurance
die	Windschutzscheibe, -n	windscreen

USEFUL PHRASES

fahren to drive; abfahren to leave, set off
einsteigen to get in; aussteigen to get out
sich anschnallen to put on one's seat belt
(voll) tanken to fill up (with petrol)
reisen to travel
hinten in the back; vorn(e) in the front

USEFUL WORDS (*masculine*)

der	Abschleppdienst	breakdown service
der	Abschleppwagen	breakdown van
der	Anhänger	trailer
der	Anlasser	starter
der	Durchgangsverkehr	through traffic
der	Fußgängerüberweg, -e	pedestrian crossing
der	Katalysator, -en	catalytic converter
der	Kreisverkehr, -e	roundabout
der	Leerlauf	neutral (gear)
der	Scheibenwischer	windscreen wiper
der	Strafzettel	(parking) ticket
der	Tachometer	speedometer
der	Verkehrsrowdy, -s	road hog
der	Wagenheber	jack

USEFUL WORDS (*neuter*)

das	Armaturenbrett, -er	dashboard
das	Ersatzreifen	spare tyre
das	Ersatzteil, -e	spare part
das	Getriebe	gearbox
das	Kat-Auto, -s	car with a catalytic converter
das	polizeiliche Kennzeichen	registration number
das	Lenkrad, ¨er	steering wheel
das	Nummernschild, -er	number plate
das	Steuerrad, ¨er	steering wheel
das	Verdeck, -e	hood
das	Verkehrsdelikt, -e	traffic offence
das	Warndreieck, -e	warning triangle

USEFUL PHRASES

gute Reise! have a good trip!
bremsen to brake; schalten to change gear
hupen to sound *or* toot the horn
überholen to overtake; sich einordnen to get into lane
abbiegen to turn off; halten to stop
abstellen to park, to switch off; abschleppen to tow away
parken to park; abschließen to lock; ankommen to arrive

USEFUL WORDS *(feminine)*

die	Abzweigung, -en	junction
die	Auffahrt, -en	slip road
die	Autovermietung, -en	car hire
die	Beleuchtung, -en	lights *(pl)*
die	Biegung, -en	bend, curve
die	Gasse, -n	alley, lane, back street
die	Geschwindigkeits-	speed limit, speed
	begrenzung, -en	restriction
die	Hupe, -n	horn, hooter
die	Karosserie, -n	bodywork, body
die	Kupplung, -en	clutch
die	Marke, -n	make *(of car)*
die	(Motor)haube, -n	bonnet
die	Politesse, -n	traffic warden
die	Stoßstange, -n	bumper
die	(Versicherungs)police, -n	insurance policy

USEFUL PHRASES

schnell fast; langsam slowly
gefährlich dangerous; kaputt broken, done
sperren to block; prüfen to check
Abstand halten to keep one's distance
in ein Auto fahren to bump into a car
das Auto reparieren lassen to have the car repaired
100 Kilometer in der Stunde machen to do 100 kilometres an hour
beschleunigen, Gas geben to accelerate
die Ampel überfahren to go through the lights at red
mir ist das Benzin ausgegangen I've run out of petrol
verbleit leaded; unverbleit, bleifrei unleaded
sich verfahren to get lost, take the wrong road
sich zurechtfinden to find one's way
trampen, per Anhalter fahren to hitch-hike
„Anlieger frei" "residents only"
„Parken verboten" "no parking"; „freihalten" "keep clear"
„Vorfahrt achten" "give way"

ESSENTIAL WORDS (masculine)

der	**Anorak, -s**	anorak
der	**Badeanzug, ̈e**	swimming or bathing costume
der	**Gürtel**	belt
der	**Handschuh, -e**	glove
der	**Kleiderschrank, ̈e**	wardrobe
der	**Knopf, ̈e**	button
der	**Mantel, ̈e**	coat, overcoat
der	**Pullover;** der **Pulli, -s**	pullover, jumper, jersey
der	**Pyjama, -s**	(pair of) pyjamas
der	**Regenmantel, ̈**	raincoat
der	**Rock, ̈e**	skirt
der	**Schlips, -e**	tie
der	**Schuh, -e**	shoe
der	**(Spazier)stock, ̈e**	walking stick
der	**Umkleideraum, -räume**	changing room

USEFUL PHRASES

ich ziehe mich an I get dressed, I put on my clothes
ich ziehe mich aus I get undressed, I take off my clothes
ich ziehe mich um I get changed, I change my clothes
tragen to wear
Hosen/einen Mantel tragen to wear trousers/a coat
seine Schuhe/seinen Mantel anziehen to put on one's shoes/coat
seine Schuhe/seinen Mantel ausziehen to take off one's shoes/coat
einen Hut tragen to wear a hat
sich (dat) den Hut aufsetzen to put on one's hat
den Hut abnehmen to take off one's hat
darf ich dieses Kleid anprobieren? may I try on this dress?
das steht Ihnen (gut) that suits you
passen to fit; groß big; klein small
das passt mir nicht that doesn't fit me; passend matching
waschen to wash; bügeln to iron
chemisch reinigen to dryclean

ESSENTIAL WORDS (feminine)

die	Badehose, -n	swimming or bathing trunks
die	Bluse, -n	blouse
die	Brille, -n	(pair of) glasses
die	Größe, -n	size
die	Handtasche, -n	handbag
die	Hose, -n	(pair of) trousers
die	Jacke, -n	jacket
die	Jeans (pl)	jeans
die	Kleidung	clothing
die	Krawatte, -n	tie
die	Lederhose, -n	(pair of) leather shorts or trousers
die	Mode, -n	fashion
die	Sandale, -n	sandal
die	Socke, -n	sock
die	Tasche, -n	pocket; bag

ESSENTIAL WORDS (neuter)

das	Abendkleid, -er	evening dress (woman's)
das	Band, ⁻er	ribbon
das	Hemd, -en	shirt
das	Kleid, -er	dress
die	Kleider (pl)	clothes, clothing
das	Nachthemd, -en	nightdress; nightshirt
das	Taschentuch, ⁻er	handkerchief
das	T-Shirt, -s	T-shirt, tee-shirt

USEFUL PHRASES

bunt coloured; kariert checked; gestreift striped
in Mode in fashion
modisch fashionable; unmodisch out of fashion
altmodisch old-fashioned; sehr schick very smart
Brustumfang (m) bust or chest measurement
Hüftweite (f) hip measurement
Kragenweite (f) collar size; Schuhgröße (f) shoe size
Taillenweite (f) waist measurement

IMPORTANT WORDS *(masculine)*

der Anzug, ⸚e	suit
der BH, -s (Büstenhalter)	bra
der Hausschuh, -e	slipper
der Hut, ⸚e	hat
der Overall, -s	(set of) overalls
der Schal, -e *or* -s	scarf
der Schlafanzug, ⸚e	(pair of) pyjamas
der Schleier	veil
der Stiefel	boot
der Strumpf, ⸚e	stocking, (long) sock
der Trainingsanzug, ⸚e	tracksuit
der Turban, -e	turban
die Turnschuhe *(pl)*	trainers, training shoes
der Unterrock, ⸚e	underskirt, petticoat

IMPORTANT WORDS *(feminine)*

die Fliege, -n	bow tie
die Freizeitkleidung	casual clothes
die Herrenkonfektion	menswear
die Modenschau, -en	fashion show
die Mütze, -n	cap
die Schultertasche, -n	shoulder bag
die Strumpfhose, -n	(pair of) tights
die Uniform, -en	uniform
die Unterhose, -n	(under)pants *(pl)*
die Unterwäsche	underwear
die Wäsche, -n	washing; (under)clothes

IMPORTANT WORDS *(neuter)*

das Blouson, -s	bomber jacket
das Jackett, -s *or* -e	jacket
das Kostüm, -e	(lady's) suit
die Shorts *(pl)*	shorts
das Sweatshirt, -s	sweatshirt
das Unterhemd, -en	vest

USEFUL WORDS (masculine)

der	**Ärmel**	sleeve
der	**Gesellschaftsanzug, ̈e**	evening dress (man's)
der	**Hosenanzug, ̈e**	trouser suit
der	**Hosenrock, ̈e**	culottes
der	**Hosenträger**	braces (pl)
der	**Jogginganzug, ̈e**	jogging suit
der	**Kragen**	collar
die	**Lumpen** (pl)	rags
der	**Morgenrock, ̈e**	dressing gown
der	**Reißverschluss, ̈e**	zip
der	**Rollkragen**	polo neck
der	**Schnürsenkel**	shoelace
der	**Smoking, -s**	dinner jacket

USEFUL WORDS (feminine)

die	**Falte, -n**	pleat
die	**Kappe, -n**	cap, hood
die	**Kragenweite, -n**	collar size
die	**Latzhose, -n**	dungarees
die	**Markenkleidung**	branded clothes (pl)
die	**Melone, -n**	bowler hat
die	**Schürze, -n**	apron
die	**Strickjacke, -n**	cardigan
die	**Tracht, -en**	costume, dress
die	**Weste, -n**	waistcoat
die	**Wolljacke, -n**	cardigan

USEFUL WORDS (neuter)

das	**Hochzeitskleid, -er**	wedding dress
das	**Kopftuch, ̈er**	headscarf, headsquare
das	**Zubehör**	accessories (pl)

USEFUL PHRASES

sich verkleiden to disguise oneself; maskiert masked
maßgeschneidert made to measure
von der Stange off the peg

beige	beige, fawn
blau	blue
braun	brown
gelb	yellow
golden	golden
grau	grey
grün	green
lila	purple
orange	orange
pink	shocking pink
rehbraun	fawn
rosa	pink
rot	red
schwarz	black
silbern	silver
veilchenblau	violet
violett	violet, purple
weiß	white
dunkelblau	dark blue
hellblau	light blue, pale blue
bläulich	bluish
himmelblau	sky blue
königsblau	royal blue
marineblau	navy blue

USEFUL PHRASES

das Blau steht ihr blue suits her
etwas blau anstreichen to paint something blue
die Farbe wechseln to change colour
bunte/dunkle Farben bright/dark colours
das Farbfernsehen colour television

SOME COLOURFUL PHRASES

was für eine Farbe hat es? what colour is it?
blau vor Kälte blue with cold
eine Fahrt ins Blaue a mystery tour
ein blaues Auge a black eye
sie hat blaue Augen she has blue eyes
braun werden to go or turn brown (*people, leaves*)
gelb vor Neid green with envy
grün und blau black and blue
die grüne Versicherungskarte green card (*for motor insurance*)
die Grünen the Green party
Rotkäppchen Little Red Riding Hood
in den roten Zahlen in the red, in debt
in den schwarzen Zahlen in the black
ein Schwarzer a black man
eine Schwarze a black woman
ein Schwarzes Brett a notice board
ein Weißer a white man
eine Weiße a white woman
das Weiße Haus the White House
schneeweiß as white as snow
leichenblass as white as a sheet

ESSENTIAL + IMPORTANT WORDS *(masculine)*

der	Bildschirm, -e	monitor, screen
der	Computer	computer
der	Cursor	cursor
der	Drucker	printer
der	Monitor, -e	monitor
der	PC, -s	PC, personal computer
der	Programmierer	(computer) programmer
der	Speicher	memory
der	Virus, Viren	virus

ESSENTIAL + IMPORTANT WORDS *(feminine)*

die	CD-ROM, -s	CD-ROM
die	Datei, -en	file
die	Diskette, -n	disk; floppy disk
die	E-Mail, -s	e-mail
die	Festplatte, -n	hard disk
die	Hardware	hardware
die	Maus, Mäuse	mouse
die	Sicherheitskopie, -n	backup (copy)
die	Software	software
die	Tastatur, -en	keyboard
die	Taste, -n	key

ESSENTIAL + IMPORTANT WORDS *(neuter)*

das	Betriebssystem, -e	operating system
das	Breitband	broadband
die	Daten *(pl)*	data
das	Fenster	window
das	Internet	Internet
das	Laufwerk, -e	drive
das	Menü, -s	menu
das	Modem, -s	modem
das	Passwort, -wörter	password
das	Popup-Menü, -s	pop-up menu
das	Programm, -e	program

USEFUL WORDS *(masculine)*

der	Ausdruck, -e	printout
der	Benutzer	user
der	Browser	browser
der	Chip, -s	chip
der	Hacker	hacker
der	Heimcomputer	home computer
der	Informatiker	computer scientist
der	Joystick, -s	joystick
der	Laserdrucker	laser printer
der	Ordner	folder
der	Papierkorb, ¨-e	trash, recycle bin
der	Programmierer	(computer) programmer
der	Provider	provider
der	Rechner	computer; calculator
der	Schrägstrich, -e	slash
der	Seitenwechsel	page break
der	Server	server
der	Spamfilter	spam filter
der	Tintenstrahldrucker	ink-jet (printer)
der	Zeilenabstand, ¨-e	line spacing

USEFUL WORDS *(feminine)*

die	Anwendung, -en	application
die	Datenbank, -en	database
die	Eingabetaste, -n	enter key
die	E-Mail-Adresse, -n	e-mail address
die	Funktion, -en	function
die	Hilfefunktion, -en	help function
die	Homepage, -s	homepage

USEFUL PHRASES

spielen to play; sich amüsieren to have fun
ein Programm schreiben to write a program
den Computer programmieren to program the computer
den Cursor bewegen to move the cursor; klicken to click
bearbeiten to edit; einfügen to insert; to paste
formatieren to format; kopieren to copy; löschen to delete

USEFUL WORDS *(feminine continued)*

die	**Informatik**	computer science, computing
die	**Internetauktion, -en**	Internet auction
die	**Leertaste, -n**	space bar
die	**Löschtaste, -n**	delete key
die	**Mausmatte, -n**	mouse pad
die	**Rechtschreibprüfung,-en**	spellchecker
die	**Schaltfläche, -n**	button
die	**Schnittstelle, -n**	interface
die	**Schriftart, -en**	font
die	**Sicherungskopie, -n**	back-up (copy)
die	**Suchmaschine, -n**	search engine
die	**Tabellenkalkulation, -en**	spreadsheet (program)
die	**Textverarbeitung, -en**	word processor
die	**Webadresse, -n**	Web address
die	**Webseite, -n**	Web page

USEFUL WORDS *(neuter)*

das	**Bildschirmgerät, -e**	VDU, visual display unit
das	**CD-ROM-Laufwerk, -e**	CD-ROM drive
das	**Computerspiel, -e**	computer game
das	**Diskettenlaufwerk, -e**	disk drive
das	**Dokument, -e**	document
das	**DVD-Laufwerk, -e**	DVD drive
das	**Interface, -s**	interface
das	**Notebook, -s**	notebook (computer)
das	**Programmieren**	(computer) programming
das	**RAM**	RAM *(random access memory)*
das	**ROM**	ROM *(read only memory)*
das	**Symbol, -e**	icon
das	**Virensuchprogramm, -e**	virus checker
das	**Zeichen**	character

USEFUL PHRASES

die Daten speichern to store the data; die Daten sichern to save the data
im Internet surfen to surf the Internet; ausdrucken to print out; mailen to e-mail
elektronisch electronic; fett bold; kursiv italic; mager roman; tragbar portable
linksbündig left adjusted; rechtsbündig right adjusted

COUNTRIES

All countries are neuter unless marked otherwise. Where an article is shown, the noun is used with the article.

	Afrika	Africa
	Asien	Asia
	Australien	Australia
	Belgien	Belgium
	Brasilien	Brazil
	Bulgarien	Bulgaria
die	**Bundesrepublik Deutschland (BRD)**	Germany
	China	China
	Dänemark	Denmark
	Deutschland	Germany
	England	England
	Europa	Europe
die	**Europäische Union (EU)**	the European Union (EU)
	Finnland	Finland
	Frankreich	France
	Großbritannien	Great Britain
	Griechenland	Greece
	Holland	Holland
	Indien	India
der	**Irak**	Iraq
der	**Iran**	Iran
	Irland	Ireland
	Italien	Italy
	Japan	Japan
	Kanada	Canada
	Korea	Korea
	Luxemburg	Luxembourg
	Mexiko	Mexico
	Neuseeland	New Zealand
die	**Niederlande** *(pl)*	the Netherlands
	Nordirland	Northern Ireland
	Norwegen	Norway
	Österreich	Austria

COUNTRIES *(continued)*

	Pakistan	Pakistan
	Polen	Poland
	Portugal	Portugal
	Rumänien	Romania
	Russland	Russia
	Saudi-Arabien	Saudi Arabia
	Schottland	Scotland
	Schweden	Sweden
die	Schweiz	Switzerland
	Skandinavien	Scandinavia
	Spanien	Spain
	Südafrika	South Africa
	Südamerika	South America
die	Tschechische Republik	the Czech Republic
die	Türkei	Turkey
	Ungarn	Hungary
das	Vereinigte Königreich	the United Kingdom
die	Vereinigten Staaten	the United States
	(mpl) (von Amerika)	(of America)
	Vietnam	Vietnam
	Wales	Wales

USEFUL PHRASES

in die Niederlande/in die Schweiz fahren to go to the Netherlands/
    to Switzerland
nach Deutschland fahren to go to Germany
ein Land, *(pl)* Länder country
die Entwicklungsländer *(pl)* developing countries
ins Ausland fahren *or* gehen to go *or* travel abroad
im Ausland sein to be abroad
ein Ausländer, eine Ausländerin a foreigner
die Hauptstadt capital
ich bin in Deutschland geboren I was born in Germany

NATIONALITIES (*masculine*)

ein	**Afrikaner**	an African
ein	**Amerikaner**	an American
ein	**Araber**	an Arab
ein	**Asiat, -en**	an Asian
ein	**Australier**	an Australian
ein	**Belgier**	a Belgian
ein	**Brasilianer**	a Brazilian
ein	**Brite, -n**	a Briton (*pl* the British)
ein	**Chinese, -n**	a Chinese
ein	**Däne, -n**	a Dane
ein	**Deutscher, -n**	a German
ein	**Engländer**	an Englishman
ein	**Europäer**	a European
ein	**Finne, -n**	a Finn
ein	**Franzose, -n**	a Frenchman
ein	**Grieche, -n**	a Greek
ein	**Holländer**	a Dutchman
ein	**Inder**	an Indian
ein	**Iraker**	an Iraqi
ein	**Iraner**	an Iranian
ein	**Ire**	an Irishman
ein	**Italiener**	an Italian
ein	**Japaner**	a Japanese
ein	**Kanadier**	a Canadian
ein	**Luxemburger**	a native of Luxemburg
ein	**Mexikaner**	a Mexican
ein	**Neuseeländer**	a New Zealander
ein	**Niederländer**	a Dutchman
ein	**Norweger**	a Norwegian
ein	**Österreicher**	an Austrian
ein	**Pole, -n**	a Pole
ein	**Portugiese, -n**	a Portuguese
ein	**Rumäne, -n**	a Romanian
ein	**Russe, -n**	a Russian
ein	**Schotte, -n**	a Scotsman, a Scot
ein	**Schwede, -n**	a Swede
ein	**Schweizer**	a Swiss
ein	**Spanier**	a Spaniard

NATIONALITIES *(masculine continued)*

ein **Türke, -n**	a Turk
ein **Ungar, -n**	a Hungarian
ein **Vietnamese, -n**	a Vietnamese
ein **Waliser**	a Welshman

The forms given above and on the following two pages are the noun forms. The corresponding adjectives begin with a small letter and end in **-isch**.

Most can be formed by changing **-er(in)** or **-ier(in)** to **-isch**.

The main exceptions are as follows: **deutsch** (German), **englisch** (English), **französisch** (French), **schweizerisch** (Swiss).

NATIONALITIES *(feminine)*

eine **Afrikanerin**	an African (girl *or* woman)
eine **Amerikanerin**	an American (girl *or* woman)
eine **Araberin**	an Arabian (girl *or* woman)
eine **Asiatin**	an Asian (girl *or* woman)
eine **Australierin**	an Australian (girl *or* woman)
eine **Belgierin**	a Belgian (girl *or* woman)
eine **Brasilianerin**	a Brazilian (girl *or* woman)
eine **Britin**	a Briton, a British girl *or* woman
eine **Chinesin**	a Chinese (girl *or* woman)
eine **Dänin**	a Dane, a Danish girl *or* woman
eine **Deutsche**	a German (girl *or* woman)
eine **Engländerin**	an Englishwoman, an English girl
eine **Europäerin**	a European (girl *or* woman)
eine **Finnin**	a Finn, a Finnish girl *or* woman
eine **Französin**	a Frenchwoman, a French girl
eine **Griechin**	a Greek, a Greek girl *or* woman
eine **Holländerin**	a Dutchwoman, a Dutch girl
eine **Inderin**	an Indian (girl *or* woman)
eine **Irakerin**	an Iraqi (girl *or* woman)
eine **Iranerin**	an Iranian (girl *or* woman)
eine **Irin**	an Irishwoman, an Irish girl
eine **Italienerin**	an Italian (girl *or* woman)

NATIONALITIES *(feminine continued)*

eine	**Japanerin**	a Japanese (girl *or* woman)
eine	**Kanadierin**	a Canadian (girl *or* woman)
eine	**Luxemburgerin**	a native of Luxemburg
eine	**Mexikanerin**	a Mexican (girl *or* woman)
eine	**Neuseeländerin**	a New Zealander, a New Zealand girl *or* woman
eine	**Niederländerin**	a Dutchwoman, a Dutch girl
eine	**Norwegerin**	a Norwegian (girl *or* woman)
eine	**Österreicherin**	an Austrian (girl *or* woman)
eine	**Polin**	a Pole, a Polish girl *or* woman
eine	**Portugiesin**	a Portuguese (girl *or* woman)
eine	**Rumänin**	a Rumanian (girl *or* woman)
eine	**Russin**	a Russian (girl *or* woman)
eine	**Schottin**	a Scotswoman, a Scots girl
eine	**Schwedin**	a Swede, a Swedish girl *or* woman
eine	**Schweizerin**	a Swiss girl *or* woman
eine	**Spanierin**	a Spaniard, a Spanish girl *or* woman
eine	**Türkin**	a Turkish girl *or* woman
eine	**Ungarin**	a Hungarian (girl *or* woman)
eine	**Vietnamesin**	a Vietnamese (girl *or* woman)
eine	**Waliserin**	a Welshwoman, a Welsh girl

USEFUL PHRASES
die Staatsangehörigkeit nationality
die Religion religion
die Muttersprache native language

ESSENTIAL WORDS (masculine)

der Bauernhof, ⁻e	farmyard, farm
der Baum, Bäume	tree
der Berg, -e	mountain, hill
der Fluss, ⁻e	river
der Gasthof, ⁻e	inn
der Grund	ground
der Hügel	hill
der Lärm	noise
der Markt, ⁻e	market
der See, -n	lake
der Stein, -e	stone, rock
der Stock, ⁻e	cane, stick
der Turm, ⁻e	tower; (church) steeple
der Wald, ⁻er	wood, forest

ESSENTIAL WORDS (neuter)

das Dorf, ⁻er	village
das Feld, -er	field
das Gasthaus, -häuser	inn
das Land, ⁻er	land; country
das Picknick, -e or -s	picnic
das Schloss, ⁻er	castle
das Tal, ⁻er	valley
das Wirtshaus, -häuser	inn

USEFUL PHRASES

aufs Land gehen to go into the country
auf dem Lande wohnen to live in the country
auf dem Bauernhof on the farm
ein Picknick machen to go for a picnic
im Freien in the open air

ESSENTIAL WORDS *(feminine)*

die **Blume, -n**	flower
die **Brücke, -n**	bridge
die **Burg, -en**	castle
die **Höhle, -n**	cave, hole
die **Jugendherberge, -n**	youth hostel
die **Kirche, -n**	church
die **Landschaft, -en**	countryside, scenery
die **Landstraße, -n**	country road
die **Luft**	air
die **Straße, -n**	road, street
die **Wiese, -n**	meadow

USEFUL PHRASES

hügelig hilly; flach flat; steil steep
ruhig peaceful
fruchtbar fertile; schlecht bad, poor
kultivieren, anbauen to cultivate, grow
fließen to flow
bummeln to wander, stroll
überqueren to cross
jagen to hunt; to shoot
in einer Jugendherberge übernachten to spend the night in a youth hostel
sich auf den Weg machen to set out, set off
der Weg zum Dorf the way to the village
in der Ferne in the distance

IMPORTANT WORDS (*masculine*)

der **Bach, ⸚e**	stream, brook
der **Bauer, -n**	farmer; peasant
der **Boden, ⸚**	ground, earth
der **Forst, -e**	forest
der **Friede(n)**	peace
der **Gipfel**	(mountain) top
der **Gummistiefel**	wellington (boot)
der **Spazierstock, ⸚e**	walking stick
der **Stiefel**	boot
der **Strom, ⸚e**	river
der **Tourist, -en**	tourist
der **Wasserfall, ⸚e**	waterfall
der **Weg, -e**	path, way, road

IMPORTANT WORDS (*feminine*)

die **Bäuerin**	lady farmer; farmer's wife; peasant
die **Bauersfrau, -en**	farmer's wife
die **Erde, -n**	earth, soil
die **Gegend, -en**	district, area
die **Heide, -n**	heath; heather
die **Landwirtschaft**	agriculture, farming
die **Talsperre, -n**	dam

IMPORTANT WORDS (*neuter*)

das **Bauernhaus, -häuser**	farmhouse
das **Fernglas, ⸚er**	(pair of) binoculars
das **Flachland**	lowlands (*pl*)
das **Gebiet, -e**	area
das **Gebirge**	mountain chain
das **Heideland**	heath
das **Heu**	hay
das **Korn**	corn, grain
das **Tor, -e**	gate
das **Ufer**	(river) bank

USEFUL WORDS (masculine)

der	Acker, ⸚	field
der	Bewohner	inhabitant
der	Dorfbewohner	villager
der	Erdboden, ⸚	ground
der	Jäger	hunter
der	Landwirt, -e	farmer
der	Pfad, -e	path
der	Schlamm	mud
der	Sumpf, ⸚e	marsh
der	Teich, -e	pond
der	Wegweiser	signpost
der	Weiher	pond, lake
der	Weiler	hamlet
der	Weinberg, -e	vineyard
der	Wipfel	treetop

USEFUL WORDS (feminine)

die	Ebene, -n	plain
die	Ernte, -n	harvest, crop
die	Falle, -n	trap
die	Gemeinde, -n	community
die	Hecke, -n	hedge
die	Jagd, -en	hunt; hunting
die	Quelle, -n	spring; source
die	Spitze, -n	tip, peak, point
die	(Wind)mühle, -n	(wind)mill

USEFUL WORDS (neuter)

das	Geräusch, -e	noise, sound
das	Getreide	grain, cereal crop
das	Grundstück, -e	estate; plot of land
das	Heidekraut	heather
das	Loch, ⸚er	hole

ESSENTIAL WORDS (masculine)

der	Ausländer	foreigner
der	Bart, ⸚e	beard
der	Herr, -en	gentleman
der	Junge, -n	boy
der	Mann, ⸚er	man
der	Mensch, -en	human being; man; person
der	Schnurrbart, ⸚e	moustache

ESSENTIAL WORDS (feminine)

die	Ähnlichkeit, -en (mit)	similarity (to)
die	Auge, -n	eye
die	Ausländerin	foreigner
die	Bewegung, -en	movement, motion
die	Brille, -n	(pair of) glasses
die	Dame, -n	lady
die	Frau, -en	woman
die	Gesichtsfarbe, -n	complexion
die	Größe, -n	height; size
die	Hautfarbe, -n	skin colour
die	Person, -en	person
die	Schönheit	beauty

ESSENTIAL WORDS (neuter)

das	Alter	age
das	Aussehen	appearance
das	Haar, -e	hair
das	Mädchen	girl

USEFUL PHRASES
ich heiße Wolfgang my name is Wolfgang
wie heißen Sie? what is your name?
jung young; alt old
wie alt sind Sie? how old are you?, what age are you?
ich bin 16 (Jahre alt) I am 16 (years old)
mittleren Alters middle-aged

USEFUL PHRASES

bärtig bearded; schnurrbärtig with a moustache
glatt rasiert clean-shaven
er sieht wie sein Vater aus/wie seine Mutter aus he looks like his
    father/his mother
er ist seinem Vater/seiner Mutter ähnlich he resembles his father/
    his mother
erkennen to recognize
gut/schlecht aussehen to look well/poorly
müde/zornig/komisch aussehen to look tired/angry/funny
ein gut aussehender Mann a handsome or good-looking man
eine schöne Frau a beautiful woman
groß tall, big; klein short, small; lang long; kurz short
ein Mann von mittlerer Größe a man of medium height
sie ist 1 Meter 70 groß she is 1 metre 70 tall
weiß white; schwarz black; gemischtrassig of mixed ethnic origins
grüne/blaue/braune Augen haben to have green/blue/brown eyes
Kontaktlinsen/eine Brille tragen to wear contact lenses/glasses
er hat blonde/dunkle/schwarze/rote/graue Haare he has blond or
    fair/dark/black/red/grey hair
rothaarig red-haired
eine Glatze bekommen to be going bald
lockiges/welliges/glattes Haar curly/wavy/straight hair
sich benehmen to behave (oneself)
weinen to cry; lachen to laugh; lächeln to smile
vor Freude lachen/weinen to laugh/cry with joy
eine gute Figur haben to have a nice figure
wie viel wiegst du? what do you weigh?
die Gewohnheit haben, etw zu tun to have a habit of doing sth
(nicht) in der Laune or in der Stimmung für etw (acc) sein (not) to be in the
    mood for sth
gut/schlecht gelaunt in a good/bad mood
auf jdn böse sein to be angry with sb
ärgern to annoy

IMPORTANT WORDS (*masculine*)

der	**Charakter**	character
der	**Gang, ⁔e**	walk, gait
der	**Mangel, ⁔**	defect, fault
der	**Zorn**	anger

IMPORTANT WORDS (*feminine*)

die	**Figur, -en**	figure
die	**Freude, -n**	joy, delight
die	**Geste, -n**	gesture
die	**Kontaktlinsen** (*pl*)	contact lenses
die	**Natur, -en**	nature
die	**Rasse, -n**	race
die	**Schüchternheit**	shyness

IMPORTANT WORDS (*neuter*)

das	**Gewicht, -e**	weight
das	**Wesen**	character, personality

USEFUL WORDS (*masculine*)

der	**Afrikaner**	African (man)
der	**Asiat, -en**	Asian (man)
der	**Ausdruck, ⁔e**	expression
der	**Faulenzer**	lazybones
der	**Gesichtszug, ⁔e**	(facial) feature
der	**Körperbau**	build
der	**Leberfleck, -e**	mole
der	**Muslim, -e**	Muslim (man)
der	**Pickel**	spot, pimple
der	**Pony, -s**	fringe
der	**Riese, -n**	giant
der	**Schönheitsfleck, -e**	beauty spot
der	**Schweiß**	sweat, perspiration
der	**Teint, -s**	complexion
der	**Turban, -e**	turban
der	**Zug, ⁔e**	feature

USEFUL WORDS *(feminine)*

die	**Afrikanerin**	African (woman)
die	**Ängstlichkeit**	nervousness
die	**Asiatin**	Asian (woman)
die	**Dauerwelle, -n**	perm
die	**Eigenschaft, -en**	quality, attribute
die	**Falte, -n**	wrinkle
die	**Faulenzerin**	lazybones
die	**Frisur, -en**	hairstyle
die	**Gestalt, -en**	figure
die	**Gewohnheit, -en**	habit
die	**Glatze, -n**	bald head
die	**Hässlichkeit**	ugliness
die	**Laune, -n**	mood, humour, temper
die	**Locke, -n**	curl
die	**Muslimin**	Muslim (woman)
die	**Narbe, -n**	scar
die	**Runzel, -n**	wrinkle
die	**Sommersprosse, -n**	freckle
die	**Stimmung, -en**	mood, frame of mind
die	**Träne, -n**	tear
die	**Wut**	fury, rage

USEFUL WORDS *(neuter)*

das	**Benehmen**	behaviour
das	**Doppelkinn, -e**	double chin
das	**Gebiss, -e**	false teeth
das	**Gefühl, -e**	feeling
das	**Gewissen**	conscience
das	**Grübchen**	dimple
das	**Kopftuch, -̈er**	headscarf
das	**(Lebe)wesen**	creature
das	**Selbstvertrauen**	self-confidence

ähnlich (+ *dat*)	similar (to), like
ängstlich	nervous, worried
auffallend	striking
blass	pale
blind	blind
böse	angry; evil
bucklig	hunch-backed
dick	fat
dumm	stupid
dunkel	dark
dünn	thin
Durchschnitts-	average
ehrlich	honest
einsam	lonely
enttäuscht	disappointed
ernst	serious
frech (zu + *dat*)	cheeky (to)
freundlich (zu + *dat*)	friendly (to), kind (to)
froh, fröhlich	glad, happy
gebräunt	tanned
geduldig	patient
geschickt	skilful, clever
glücklich	happy
grausam	cruel
groß	tall; big
gutmütig	good-natured
hässlich	ugly
hell	fair (*skin*); light
homosexuell	homosexual
hübsch	pretty
intelligent	intelligent
klein	small
klug	clever
komisch	funny
kräftig	strong
kurz	short
kurzsichtig/weitsichtig	short-sighted/long-sighted
lächerlich	ridiculous
lahm	lame

lang	long
lesbisch	lesbian
mager	skinny, thin, lean
mürrisch	sullen
nachlässig	careless
nackt	bare, naked
nervös	nervous
nett	neat; nice
neugierig	curious, nosy
pickelig	spotty
reizend	charming
rund	round
schlank	slender
schön	beautiful
schüchtern	shy
schwach	weak
schwarz	black
seltsam	strange
sorgfältig	careful, painstaking
stark	strong
stolz (auf + acc)	proud (of)
streng	hard, harsh; strict
sympathisch	nice, likeable
tapfer	brave
taub	deaf
traurig	sad
unartig	naughty
ungeschickt	clumsy, awkward
vernünftig	sensible
verrückt	crazy, mad
verschieden	different
vorsichtig	careful, cautious
weise	wise
weiß	white
winzig	tiny
zornig	angry
zufrieden (mit + dat)	pleased (with)

ESSENTIAL WORDS *(masculine)*

der	**Bleistift, -e**	pencil
der	**Computer**	computer
der	**Direktor, -en**	principal, headmaster
die	**Ferien** *(pl)*	holidays
der	**Fernseher**	television
der	**Filzstift, -e**	felt-tip pen
der	**Freund, -e**	friend
der	**Informatikunterricht**	computer studies
der	**Kindergarten, ⁻**	nursery school
der	**Klassenlehrer**	form teacher
der	**Kugelschreiber**	ballpoint pen
der	**Kuli, -s**	Biro®, ballpoint pen
der	**Lehrer**	(school)teacher
der	**Preis, -e**	prize
der	**Prüfer**	examiner
der	**Rechner**	calculator; computer
der	**Schreibtisch, -e**	desk
der	**Schulanfang**	beginning of term
der	**Schüler**	schoolboy, pupil, student
der	**Schulfreund, -e**	schoolfriend
der	**Schulhof, ⁻e**	playground
der	**Schulkamerad, -en**	schoolfriend
der	**Speisesaal, -säle**	dining hall
der	**Spielplatz, ⁻e**	playground
der	**Stundenplan, ⁻e**	timetable
der	**Taschenrechner**	pocket calculator
der	**Test, -s**	test
der	**Unterricht, -e**	instruction; *(pl)* lessons
der	**Versuch, -e**	experiment

ESSENTIAL WORDS *(feminine)*

die **Abschlussprüfung**	final exam
die **Antwort, -en**	answer
die **Arbeit, -en**	work; test
die **Aufgabe, -n**	exercise, task
die **Bibliothek, -en**	library
die **Biologie**	biology
die **Chemie**	chemistry
die **Direktorin**	headmistress *(of secondary school)*
die **Erdkunde**	geography
die **Frage, -n**	question
die **Freundin**	friend
die **Gemeinschaftskunde**	social studies
die **Geografie**	geography
die **Gesamtschule, -n**	comprehensive school
die **Geschichte, -n**	history; story
die **Grundschule, -n**	primary school
die **Gruppe, -n**	group
die **Handarbeit**	handicrafts; needlework
die **Hauptschule, -n**	secondary school
die **Hausaufgabe, -n**	homework
die **Karte, -n**	map; card
die **Klasse, -n**	class, form
die **Klassenarbeit, -en**	test
die **Klassenfahrt, -en**	(class) trip, outing
die **Klassenlehrerin**	form teacher
die **Kreide**	chalk
die **Kunst**	art
die **Lehrerin**	(school)teacher
die **Mappe, -n**	briefcase; folder
die **Mathematik; die Mathe**	mathematics, maths
die **Mittagspause, -n**	lunch break
die **Musik**	music
die **Pause, -n**	break, interval
die **Physik**	physics

USEFUL PHRASES

die Schule besuchen to attend school
in der Schule at school
ich gehe in die Schule I'm going to school
arbeiten to work
aufpassen to pay attention; zuhören to listen
lernen to learn; studieren to study; vergessen to forget
lesen to read; schreiben to write; sprechen to speak
sprichst du Deutsch? do you speak German?
seit wie vielen Jahren lernen Sie Deutsch? how many years have you been
  learning German?
ich lerne seit 3 Jahren Deutsch I've been learning German for 3 years
lehren, unterrichten to teach
ich möchte Lehrer werden I'd like to be a teacher
der Französischlehrer the French teacher (*teacher of French*)
eine Prüfung machen to sit an exam
das Abitur machen to sit one's A-levels (*approx*)
wiederholen to repeat; to revise
mündlich oral; schriftlich written
eine Prüfung bestehen/nicht bestehen to pass/fail an exam
den ersten Preis gewinnen to win first prize
durchfallen to fail
sitzen bleiben to repeat a year
Fortschritte machen to make progress
versetzen to move *or* put up
die Schule verlassen to leave school
klug clever; intelligent intelligent; dumm stupid
fragen to ask; antworten to answer, reply
jdm eine Frage stellen to ask sb a question
eine Frage beantworten to answer a question

ESSENTIAL WORDS *(feminine continued)*

die **Prüfung, -en**	exam, examination
die **Realschule, -n**	secondary school
die **(höhere) Schule, (-n) -n**	(secondary) school
die **Schülerin**	schoolgirl, pupil; student
die **Schulfreundin** or	schoolfriend
die **Schulkameradin**	
die **Schultasche, -n**	satchel, school bag
die **Schuluniform, -en**	school uniform
die **Seite, -n**	page
die **Sozialkunde**	social studies
die **Tafel, -n**	blackboard
die **Technik**	technology
die **Tinte**	ink
die **Turnhalle, -n**	gym, gymnasium
die **Universität, -en; die Uni**	university

ESSENTIAL WORDS *(neuter)*

das **Buch, ̈er**	book
das **Deutsch**	German
das **Englisch**	English
das **Examen, -** or **Examina**	exam, examination
das **Französisch**	French
das **Gymnasium, -ien**	grammar school
das **Klassenzimmer**	classroom, schoolroom
das **Lineal, -e**	ruler
das **Papier, -e**	paper
das **(Schul)fach, ̈er**	(school) subject
das **(Schul)heft, -e**	exercise book
das **Semester**	term (2 *per year*)
das **Spanish**	Spanish
das **technische Zeichnen**	technical drawing
das **Trimester**	term (3 *per year*)
das **Turnen**	P.E.; gymnastics
das **Werken**	handicrafts
das **Wörterbuch, ̈er**	dictionary

IMPORTANT WORDS (*masculine*)

der	Austausch, -e	exchange
der	Buchstabe, -n	letter of alphabet
der	Erfolg, -e	success
der	Ethikunterricht	ethics
der	Fehler	mistake, error; fault
der	Hochschüler	college student
der	Klassenkamerad, -en	classmate
der	Klassensprecher	form prefect
der	Kurs, -e	course
der	Mitschüler	classmate, schoolmate
der	Radiergummi, -s	rubber, eraser
der	Rektor, -en	headmaster (*primary*); rector
der	Schlafsaal, -säle	dormitory
der	Schülerlotse, -n	*pupil who helps with school crossing patrol*
der	Student, -en	student
der	Zettel	piece of paper; note; form

IMPORTANT WORDS (*neuter*)

das	Abitur	German school-leaving certificate/exam
das	Bestehen	pass (*in exam*)
das	Blatt, ¨er	sheet (*of paper*)
das	Diplom, -e	diploma
das	Ergebnis, -se	result (*of exam*)
das	Italienisch	Italian
das	Klassenbuch, ¨er	class register
das	Latein	Latin
das	Lehrerzimmer	staff room
das	Pflichtfach, ¨er	compulsory subject
das	Rechnen	arithmetic
das	(Schul)zeugnis, -se	(school) report
das	(Sprach)labor, -e	(language) lab
das	Vokabular	vocabulary
das	Wahlfach, ¨er	option, optional subject
das	Zeichnen	drawing (*subject*)

IMPORTANT WORDS *(feminine)*

die	Algebra	algebra
die	Aula, Aulen *or* -s	assembly hall
die	Berufsschule, -n	vocational *or* trade school
die	Fach(hoch)schule, -n	technical college
die	Fremdsprache, -n	foreign language
die	Ganztagsschule, -n	all-day school *or* schooling
die	Garderobe, -n	cloakroom
die	gemischte Schule, -n -n	mixed school, co-ed
die	Geometrie	geometry
die	Grammatik	grammar
die	Halbtagsschule, -n	half-day school
die	Hochschule, -n	college; university
die	Klassenkameradin	classmate
die	Lehre	teaching
die	Leistung, -en	achievement
die	Methode, -n	method
die	Mitschülerin	classmate, schoolmate
die	mittlere Reife	intermediate school-leaving certificate/exam
die	Nachhilfe	private coaching *or* tuition
die	Naturwissenschaft, -en	natural history
die	Note, -n	mark, grade
die	Oberstufe, -n	upper school
die	Reihe, -n	row (*of seats etc*)
die	Rektorin	headmistress (*primary*)
die	Religion	religion
die	Schülermitverwaltung, -en (SMV)	school *or* student council
die	Sprache, -n	language
die	neueren Sprachen (*pl*)	modern languages
die	Strafarbeit, -en	punishment exercise
die	Studentin	student
die	technische Hochschule, -n -n	technical college
die	Übersetzung, -en	translation
die	Übung, -en	practice; exercise
die	Zeichnung, -en	drawing (*piece of work*)

USEFUL WORDS *(masculine)*

die Abwesenden *(pl)*	absentees
die Anwesenden *(pl)*	those present
der Aufsatz, ¨e	composition, essay
der Aufsichtsschüler	prefect
der Bericht, -e	report
der Bleistiftspitzer	pencil sharpener
der Drehbleistift, -e	propelling pencil
der Federhalter	(fountain) pen
die Fortschritte *(pl)*	progress
der Füllfederhalter; der Füller	fountain pen
der Gang, ¨e	corridor
der Gesang	singing
der Internatsschüler	boarder
der Irrtum, ¨er	error
der Klecks, -e	blot, stain
der Religionsunterricht	religious education
der Satz, ¨e	sentence
der Tageslichtprojektor, -en	overhead projector
der Tagesschüler	day-boy
der Vortrag, ¨e	talk, lecture

USEFUL PHRASES

schwierig difficult; einfach easy
interessant interesting; langweilig boring
faul lazy; fleißig hard-working; streng strict
mein Lieblingsfach my favourite subject
letztes Jahr habe ich einen Austausch gemacht I did an exchange last year
schulfrei haben to have a day off
hitzefrei haben to have a day off because of very hot weather

USEFUL WORDS (*feminine*)

die	Aktentasche, -n	briefcase
die	Aufsichtsschülerin	prefect
die	Dichtung	poetry
die	Doppelstunde, -n	double period
die	Erziehung	education, schooling
die	Handelsschule, -n	commercial college
die	Hauswirtschaft	home economics
die	Internatsschülerin	boarder
die	Kantine, -n	canteen
die	Lektion, -en	lesson, unit
die	Lektüre, -n	reading
die	pädagogische Hochschule, -n -n (PH)	College of Education
die	Preisverleihung, -en	prize-giving
die	Rechtschreibung	spelling
die	Regel, -n	rule
die	Tagesschülerin	day-girl
die	Vorlesung, -en	lecture

USEFUL WORDS (*neuter*)

das	Benehmen	behaviour, conduct
das	Diktat, -e	dictation
das	Griechisch	Greek
das	Internat, -e	boarding school
das	Nachsitzen	detention
das	Notizbuch, ⁼er	jotter; notebook
das	Pult, -e	desk
das	Russisch	Russian
das	Studenten(wohn)heim, -e	students' hall of residence
das	Tonbandgerät, -e	tape recorder

USEFUL PHRASES

abschreiben to copy
die Schule schwänzen to skip school
bestrafen to punish; loben to praise
jdn nachsitzen lassen to keep sb in (after school)

ESSENTIAL WORDS *(masculine)*

der **Abfall, ⸚e**	waste
der **Baum, Bäume**	tree
der **Berg, -e**	hill, mountain
der **Energieverbrauch**	energy consumption
der **Fisch, -e**	fish
der **Fluss, ⸚e**	river
der **Müll**	rubbish, refuse
der **Regen**	rain
der **saure Regen**	acid rain
der **Schadstoff, -e**	harmful substance
der **See, -n**	lake
der **Smog**	smog
der **Umweltschutz**	conservation
der **Strand, ⸚e**	beach
der **Wald, ⸚er**	forest, wood

ESSENTIAL WORDS *(feminine)*

die **Atmosphäre**	atmosphere
die **Blume, -n**	flower
die **Fabrik, -en**	factory
die **Flasche, -n**	bottle
die **Frage, -n**	question
die **globale Erwärmung**	global warming
die **Insel, -n**	island
die **Krise, -n**	crisis
die **Luft**	air
die **Ozonschicht**	ozone layer
die **See, -n**	sea
die **Temperatur, -en**	temperature
die **Welt**	world
die **Windenergie**	wind energy
die **Windfarm, -en**	wind farm
die **Zeit, -en**	time
die **Zeitschrift, -en**	magazine
die **Zeitung, -en**	newspaper

ESSENTIAL WORDS *(neuter)*

das	**Auto, -s**	car
das	**Benzin**	petrol
das	**Essen**	food
das	**Gas, -e**	gas
das	**Gemüse**	vegetables
das	**Glas**	glass
das	**Land, ̈er**	country
das	**Meer, -e**	ocean; sea
das	**Obst**	fruit
das	**Ozonloch, ̈er**	hole in the ozone layer
das	**Schwermetall, -e**	heavy metal
das	**Tier, -e**	animal
das	**Treibgas, -e**	propellant
das	**Waldsterben**	dying of the forests
das	**Wasser**	water
das	**Wetter**	weather

USEFUL PHRASES

eine Weltreise machen to go round the world

das höchste/größte/schönste ... der Welt the highest/biggest/ most beautiful ... in the world

in der Zukunft in future

aussterben to become extinct

verschmutzen to pollute

zerstören to destroy

verunreinigen to contaminate

etw verbieten to ban sth

retten to save

wiederaufbereiten to reprocess

wiederverwerten, recyceln to recycle

biologisch abbaubar biodegradable

umweltfreundlich environment-friendly

umweltschädlich harmful to the environment

grün green; ökologisch ecological

organisch organic; bleifrei unleaded

IMPORTANT WORDS (masculine)

die	Grünen (pl)	the Greens
der	Kanal, Kanäle	canal
der	Mond	moon
der	Müllabladeplatz, ⁻e	rubbish tip or dump
der	Planet, -en	planet
die	tropischen Regenwälder (pl)	tropical rainforests
der	Strom, ⁻e	river

IMPORTANT WORDS (feminine)

die	Chemikalien (pl)	chemicals
die	Erde	the earth
die	Gegend, -en	region, area
die	Hitze	heat
die	Katastrophe, -n	catastrophe
die	Kernkraft	nuclear power
die	Küste, -n	coast
die	Lösung, -en	solution
die	Pflanze, -n	plant
die	Solaranlage, -n	solar power plant
die	Sprühdose, -n	aerosol
die	Wiederverwertung	recycling, reprocessing
die	Zukunft	future

IMPORTANT WORDS (neuter)

das	Aluminium	aluminium
das	Deodorant -s or -e	deodorant
das	Gebiet, -e	area
das	Kernkraftwerk, -e	nuclear power station
das	Klima, -s or -te	climate
das	Ökosystem	ecosystem
das	Produkt, -e	product; (pl) produce
das	Recycling	recycling
das	Spülmittel	washing-up liquid
das	Waschmittel	detergent
das	Waschpulver	washing powder

USEFUL WORDS (masculine)

die	Bodenschätze (pl)	mineral resources
der	Bohrturm, ⸚e	drilling or oil rig
der	Brennstoff, -e	fuel (for heating)
der	Dieselkraftstoff	diesel oil
der	Elektrosmog	electromagnetic radiation
der	FCKW, -s	CFC
der	Ökologe, -n	ecologist
der	Ozean, -e	ocean
der	Recyclinghof, ⸚e	recycling plant
der	Schaden, ⸚	damage, harm
der	Treibhauseffekt	greenhouse effect
der	Treibstoff, -e	fuel (for vehicles)
der	Umweltschützer	conservationist, environmentalist

USEFUL WORDS (feminine)

die	Lärmbelästigung	noise pollution
die	Luftverschmutzung	air pollution
die	Mülldeponie, -n	waste disposal site
die	Ökologin	ecologist
die	Steuer, -n	tax
die	Umwelt	environment
die	(Umwelt)verschmutzung	(environmental) pollution
die	Wiederaufarbeitungsanlage, -n	reprocessing plant
die	Windkraft	wind power
die	Wüste, -n	desert

USEFUL WORDS (neuter)

das	Abgas	exhaust fumes
die	Abwässer (pl)	sewage
das	Altpapier	waste paper
das	Erdbeben	earthquake
das	Loch, ⸚er	hole
das	Weltall	universe

ESSENTIAL WORDS *(masculine)*

	Alte(r), -n	old man/woman
der	Babysitter	babysitter
der	Bruder, ⸚	brother
die	Eltern *(pl)*	parents
	Erwachsene(r), -n	grown-up, adult
der	Familienname, -n	surname
der	Freund, -e	friend
die	Geschwister *(pl)*	brothers and sisters
die	Großeltern *(pl)*	grandparents
der	Großvater, ⸚	grandfather
der	Junge, -n	boy
die	Leute *(pl)*	people
der	Mädchenname, -n	maiden name
der	Mann, ⸚er	man; husband
der	junge Mann, -n ⸚er	youth, young man
der	Mensch, -en	human being, person
der	Name, -n	name
der	Onkel	uncle
der	Opa, -s; der Opi, -s	grandpa
der	Sohn, ⸚e	son
der	Vater, ⸚	father
der	Vati, -s	dad, daddy
der	Vorname, -n	first name, Christian name
der	Zwilling, -e	twin
der	Zwillingsbruder, ⸚	twin brother

USEFUL PHRASES

ich heiße Karl my name is Karl

ich bin 17 (Jahre alt) I am 17 (years old)

ich bin 1986 geboren I was born in 1986

wie heißt du? – wie alt bist du? what's your name? – how old are you?

männlich male; weiblich female

kennen to know; kennenlernen to get to know

vorstellen to introduce; erinnern (an + *acc*) to remind (of)

unsere Familie stammt aus Polen our family comes from Poland

wir wohnen jetzt in Österreich we live in Austria now

ESSENTIAL WORDS *(feminine)*

die	**Dame, -n**	lady
die	**Familie, -n**	family
die	**Frau, -en**	woman; wife
die	**Freundin**	friend
die	**Großmutter, ̈**	grandmother
die	**Hausfrau, -en**	housewife
die	**Mutter, ̈**	mother
die	**Mutti, -s**	mum, mummy
die	**Oma, -s;** die **Omi, -s**	granny
die	**Person, -en**	person
die	**Schwester, -n**	sister
die	**Tante, -n**	aunt
die	**Tochter, ̈**	daughter
die	**Zwillingsschwester, -n**	twin sister

ESSENTIAL WORDS *(neuter)*

das	**Alter**	age; old age
das	**Baby, -s**	baby
das	**Einzelkind, -er**	only child
das	**Fräulein**	young lady
das	**Kind, -er**	child
das	**Mädchen**	(young) girl
das	**Paar, -e**	couple

USEFUL PHRASES

verlobt engaged; verheiratet married
ledig single; geschieden divorced
meine Eltern leben getrennt my parents are separated
sich verloben to get engaged; sich verheiraten to get married
sich scheiden lassen to get divorced
älter/jünger als ich older/younger than me
die ganze Familie the whole family
bei uns at our place, at our house
mein Großvater ist 1990 gestorben my grandfather died in 1990
tot dead; streiten to quarrel; sich vertragen to get along

IMPORTANT WORDS *(masculine)*

der	Austauschpartner	partner *(in an exchange)*
	Bekannte(r), -n	acquaintance
der	Cousin, -s	cousin
der	Ehemann, ̈-er	married man; husband
der	Enkel	grandson; *(pl)* grandchildren
	Jugendliche(r), -n	teenager, young person
der	Nachbar, -n	neighbour
der	Nachname, -n	surname
der	Neffe, -n	nephew
der	Rentner	(old age) pensioner
der	Schwiegersohn, ̈-e	son-in-law
der	Schwiegervater, ̈-	father-in-law
	Verlobte(r), -n	fiancé/fiancée
	Verwandte(r), -n	relation, relative
der	Vetter, -n	cousin
der	Witwer	widower

IMPORTANT WORDS *(feminine)*

die	Cousine, -n	cousin
die	Ehefrau, -en	married woman; wife
die	Enkelin	granddaughter
die	Jugend	youth *(stage of life)*
die	Kusine, -n	cousin
die	Nachbarin	neighbour
die	Nichte, -n	niece
die	Rentnerin	(old age) pensioner
die	Schwiegermutter, ̈-	mother-in-law
die	Schwiegertochter, ̈-	daughter-in-law
die	Witwe, -n	widow

IMPORTANT WORDS *(neuter)*

das	Au-pair-Mädchen	au pair
das	Ehepaar, -e	married couple
das	Enkelkind, -er	grandchild
das	Kindermädchen	nanny

USEFUL WORDS (masculine)

der	Bräutigam, -e	bridegroom
die	Drillinge (pl)	triplets
der	Elternteil, -e	parent
der	Geburtsort, -e	place of birth
der	Junggeselle, -n	bachelor
die	Jungverheirateten (pl)	newly-weds
der	Pate, -n	godfather
der	Rufname, -n	first name, usual name
der	Säugling, -e	baby, infant
der	Schwager, ⸚	brother-in-law
der	Spitzname, -n	nickname
der	Stiefbruder, ⸚	stepbrother
der	Stiefvater, ⸚	stepfather
der	Vorfahr, -en	ancestor
der	Vormund, -e or ⸚er	guardian
der	Zuname, -n	surname

USEFUL WORDS (feminine)

die	Braut, Bräute	bride
die	Hochzeit, -en	wedding
die	alte Jungfer, -n -n	spinster, old maid
die	Junggesellin	unmarried woman
die	Patin	godmother
die	Schwägerin	sister-in-law
die	Stiefmutter, ⸚	stepmother
die	Stiefschwester, -n	stepsister
die	Waise, -n	orphan

USEFUL WORDS (neuter)

das	Geburtsdatum, -daten	date of birth
das	Greisenalter	(extreme) old age
das	Waisenhaus, -häuser	orphanage
das	Weib, -er	woman (old-fashioned or pejorative)

ESSENTIAL WORDS *(masculine)*

der	**Bauer, -n**	farmer; peasant, countryman
der	**Bauernhof, ⁼e**	farm, farmyard
der	**Hahn, ⁼e**	cock, rooster
der	**Hügel**	hill
der	**Hund, -e**	dog
der	**Landarbeiter**	farm labourer
der	**Markt, ⁼e**	market
der	**Wald, ⁼er**	wood, forest

ESSENTIAL WORDS *(feminine)*

die	**Bäuerin**	lady farmer; farmer's wife; peasant
die	**Bauersfrau, -en**	farmer's wife
die	**Ente, -n**	duck
die	**Erde**	earth, soil
die	**Gans, ⁼e**	goose
die	**Henne, -n**	hen
die	**(Heu)gabel, -n**	pitchfork
die	**Katze, -n**	cat
die	**Wiese, -n**	meadow

ESSENTIAL WORDS *(neuter)*

das	**Dorf, ⁼er**	village
das	**Feld, -er**	field
das	**Kalb, ⁼er**	calf
das	**Land, ⁼er**	land; country
das	**Tier, -e**	animal

USEFUL PHRASES

auf einem Bauernhof wohnen to live on a farm
Ferien auf dem Bauernhof farm holidays
der Bauer sorgt für die Tiere the farmer looks after the animals
die Felder pflügen to plough the fields
die Ernte einbringen to bring in the harvest *or* the crops
zur Erntezeit at harvest-time

IMPORTANT WORDS *(masculine)*

der **Bach, ⁻e**	stream, brook
der **Boden, ⁻**	ground, earth; floor; loft
der **Bulle, -n**	bull
der **Lieferwagen**	van
der **Ochse, -n**	ox
der **Ökobauer, -n**	organic farmer
der **Puter**	turkey(-cock)
der **Traktor, -en**	tractor
der **Weizen**	wheat
der **Zaun, Zäune**	fence

IMPORTANT WORDS *(feminine)*

die **Feldmaus, -mäuse**	fieldmouse
die **Heide, -n**	heath
die **Herde, -n**	herd; flock
die **Kuh, ⁻e**	cow
die **Landschaft, -en**	countryside, scenery
die **Landwirtschaft**	agriculture, farming
die **Milchkanne, -n**	milk churn
die **Ökobäuerin**	organic farmer
die **Pute, -n**	turkey(-hen)

IMPORTANT WORDS *(neuter)*

das **Bauernhaus, -häuser**	farmhouse
das **Gebäude**	building
das **Heu**	hay
das **Huhn, ⁻er**	chicken, hen; *(pl)* poultry
das **Hühnerhaus, -häuser**	henhouse
das **Korn, ⁻er**	corn, grain
das **Lamm, ⁻er**	lamb
das **Pferd, -e**	horse
das **Schaf, -e**	sheep
das **Schwein, -e**	pig
das **Stroh**	straw

USEFUL WORDS (*masculine*)

der	Acker, ⸚	field
der	Brunnen	well
der	Dünger	dung, manure; fertilizer
der	Eimer	bucket, pail
der	Esel	donkey
der	Graben, ⸚	ditch
der	Hafer	oats (*pl*)
der	Hase, -n	hare
der	Haufen	heap, pile
der	Heuboden, ⸚	hayloft
der	Karren	cart
der	Kuhstall, ⸚e	cowshed, byre
der	Landwirt, -e	farmer
der	Mähdrescher	combine harvester
der	Mais	maize
der	Pferdestall, ⸚e	stable
der	Pflug, ⸚e	plough
der	Roggen	rye
der	Schäfer	shepherd
der	Schäferhund, -e	sheepdog, German shepherd
der	Schlamm	mud
der	Schuppen	shed
der	Stall, ⸚e	stable; sty; (hen)house
der	Stapel	pile
der	Staub	dust
der	Stier, -e	bull
der	Teich, -e	pond
der	Truthahn, ⸚e	turkey(-cock)
der	Widder	ram

USEFUL WORDS *(feminine)*

die	**Ernte, -n**	harvest, crop
die	**Erntezeit, -en**	harvest (time)
die	**Furche, -n**	furrow
die	**Garbe, -n**	sheaf
die	**Gerste**	barley
die	**Kleie**	bran
die	**Leiter, -n**	ladder
die	**Scheune, -n**	barn
die	**Vogelscheuche, -n**	scarecrow
die	**Weide, -n**	pasture
die	**(Wind)mühle, -n**	(wind)mill
die	**Ziege, -n**	goat

USEFUL WORDS *(neuter)*

das	**Gatter**	gate; railing
das	**Geflügel**	poultry
das	**Geschirr, -e**	harness
das	**Getreide**	cereals, grain
das	**Küken**	chicken, chick
das	**(Rind)vieh**	cattle *(pl)*, livestock
das	**Zugpferd, -e**	carthorse

USEFUL PHRASES

genmanipulierte Lebensmittel **genetically modified food**
organisch **organic**
Eier aus Freilandhaltung **free-range eggs**
aus biologischem Anbau **organically grown**

ESSENTIAL + IMPORTANT WORDS *(masculine)*

der	Fisch, -e	fish
der	Goldfisch, -e	goldfish
der	Schwanz, ⁝e	tail

USEFUL WORDS *(masculine)*

der	Aal, -e	eel
der	Floh, ⁝e	flea
der	Flügel	wing
der	Frosch, ⁝e	frog
der	Hai(fisch), -e	shark
der	Hecht, -e	pike
der	Hering, -e	herring
der	Hummer	lobster
der	Kabeljau, -e *or* -s	cod
der	Käfer	beetle
der	Krebs, -e	crab; crayfish
der	Lachs, -e	salmon
der	Maikäfer	cockchafer
der	Marienkäfer	ladybird
der	Nachtfalter	moth
der	Schellfisch, -e	haddock
der	Schmetterling, -e	butterfly
der	Stich, -e	sting
der	Thunfisch, -e	tuna fish
der	Tintenfisch, -e	(small) octopus, squid
der	Weißfisch, -e	whiting
der	Wurm, ⁝er	worm

ESSENTIAL + IMPORTANT WORDS *(neuter)*

das	Insekt, -en	insect
das	Schalentier, -e	shellfish
das	Wasser	water

USEFUL PHRASES

im Wasser schwimmen to swim in the water
in der Luft fliegen to fly in the air
„Angeln verboten" "no fishing"

ESSENTIAL + IMPORTANT WORDS *(feminine)*

die	**Biene, -n**	bee
die	**Fliege, -n**	fly
die	**Forelle, -n**	trout
die	**Luft**	air
die	**Sardine, -n**	sardine
die	**Wespe, -n**	wasp

USEFUL WORDS *(feminine)*

die	**Ameise, -n**	ant
die	**Auster, -n**	oyster
die	**Flosse, -n**	fin
die	**Garnele, -n**	shrimp; prawn
die	**Grille, -n**	cricket
die	**Heuschrecke, -n**	grasshopper
die	**Hornisse, -n**	hornet
die	**Kaulquappe, -n**	tadpole
die	**Kiemen** *(pl)*	gills
die	**Krabbe, -n**	shrimp; prawn
die	**Languste, -n**	crayfish
die	**Libelle, -n**	dragonfly
die	**(Mies)muschel, -n**	mussel
die	**Motte, -n**	moth
die	**Mücke, -n**	midge
die	**Qualle, -n**	jellyfish
die	**Raupe, -n**	caterpillar
die	**Schmeißfliege, -n**	bluebottle
die	**Schuppe, -n**	scale
die	**Seezunge, -n**	sole
die	**Seidenraupe, -n**	silkworm
die	**Spinne, -n**	spider
die	**Stechmücke, -n**	mosquito
die	**Wanze, -n**	bug

USEFUL PHRASES
stechen to sting
die Biene/die Wespe sticht the bee/the wasp stings
die Mücke sticht the midge bites

ESSENTIAL WORDS (masculine)

der	Alkohol	alcohol
der	(Apfel)saft, ̈-e	(apple) juice
der	Apfelstrudel	apple strudel
der	Apfelwein, -e	cider
der	Appetit, -e	appetite
der	Aufschnitt, -e	cold meats
der	Becher	mug; tumbler
die	Chips (pl)	crisps
der	Durst	thirst
der	Eintopf, ̈-e	stew
der	Essig	vinegar
der	Fisch, -e	fish
der	Honig	honey
der	Hunger	hunger
der	Imbiss, -e	snack
der	Joghurt, -s	yoghurt
der	Kaffee	coffee
der	Kakao, -s	cocoa
der	Käse	cheese
der	Keks, -e	biscuit
der	Kellner	waiter
der	Kuchen	cake
der	Löffel	spoon
der	Nachtisch, -e	dessert, sweet
der	Orangensaft	orange juice
der	Pfeffer	pepper
der	Reis	rice
der	Salat, -e	salad
der	Schinken	ham
der	Schnellimbiss, -e	snack bar
der	Senf, -e	mustard
der	Sprudel	sparkling mineral water
der	Tee, -s	tea
der	Teller	plate
der	Tisch, -e	table
der	Wein, -e	wine
der	Zucker	sugar

USEFUL PHRASES

essen to eat; trinken to drink

könnte ich bitte eine Cola haben? could I have a Coke please?

wie wär's mit einem Apfelsaft? do you fancy an apple juice?

bezahlen bitte! the bill please!

schlucken to swallow; schmecken to taste (good)

probieren to try

das schmeckt ihm he likes it

schmeckt Ihnen der Wein? do you like the wine?

das schmeckt scheußlich! that tastes dreadful!

ich esse gern Käse I like (eating) cheese

ich trinke gern Tee I like (drinking) tea

ich mag Käse/Tee nicht, ich mag keinen Käse/Tee I don't like cheese/tea

ich esse lieber Brot/trinke lieber Bier I prefer bread/beer

hungrig sein, Hunger haben to be hungry

durstig sein, Durst haben to be thirsty

ich sterbe vor Hunger! I'm starving!

hast du schon gegessen? have you eaten yet?

frühstücken to have breakfast

vorbereiten to prepare; kochen to cook; backen to bake; braten to fry;
   grillen to grill; würzen to season

paniert in breadcrumbs

schneiden to cut; streichen to spread

einschenken to pour (*tea etc*)

bitten um to ask for; reichen to pass, hand on

Mahlzeit!, guten Appetit! enjoy your meal!

bedienen Sie sich!, nehmen Sie sich! help yourselves!

alkoholisch alcoholic; alkoholfrei non-alcoholic

den Tisch decken/abräumen to lay *or* set/clear the table

abwaschen, (das Geschirr) spülen to wash up, do the dishes

abtrocknen to dry the dishes

ESSENTIAL WORDS *(feminine)*

die	**Bedienung**	service; service charge
die	**Bestellung, -en**	order
die	**Bockwurst, -würste**	*type of pork sausage*
die	**(Braten)soße, -n**	gravy
die	**Bratwurst, -würste**	grilled *or* fried sausage
die	**Butter**	butter
die	**Cola**	Coke®
die	**Currywurst, -würste**	curried sausage
die	**Dose, -n**	box; tin, can
die	**Erfrischung, -en**	refreshment
die	**Flasche, -n**	bottle
die	**Frucht, ̈e**	(piece of) fruit
die	**Gabel, -n**	fork
die	**Imbissstube, -n**	snack bar
die	**Kaffeekanne, -n**	coffee pot
die	**Kartoffel, -n**	potato
die	**Kellnerin**	waitress
die	**Leberwurst**	liver sausage
die	**Limonade, -n, die Limo**	lemonade
die	**Mahlzeit, -en**	meal
die	**Margarine, -n**	margarine
die	**Milch**	milk
die	**Nachspeise, -n**	dessert, sweet
die	**Pizza, -s**	pizza
die	**kalte Platte, -n -n**	cold meal
die	**Portion, -en**	portion, helping
die	**Praline, -n**	*(individual)* chocolate
die	**Rechnung, -en**	bill
die	**Sahne**	cream
die	**Salzkartoffeln** *(pl)*	boiled potatoes
die	**Schlagsahne**	whipped cream
die	**Schokolade, -n**	chocolate
die	**Soße, -n**	sauce
die	**Speisekarte, -n**	menu
die	**Suppe, -n**	soup
die	**Tageskarte, -n**	today's menu
die	**Tasse, -n**	cup

ESSENTIAL WORDS *(neuter)*

das	**Abendbrot**	supper
das	**Abendessen**	evening meal
das	**Bier, -e**	beer
das	**Bonbon, -s**	sweet, sweetie
das	**(Brat)hähnchen**	(roast) chicken
das	**Brot, -e**	bread; loaf
ein	**belegtes Brot, -n -e**	open sandwich
das	**Brötchen**	(bread) roll
das	**Butterbrot, -e**	piece of bread and butter
das	**Café, -s**	café
das	**Ei, -er**	egg
das	**Eis**	ice cream
das	**Essen**	meal
das	**Feuerzeug, -e**	lighter
das	**Fleisch**	meat
das	**Frühstück, -e**	breakfast
das	**Gemüse**	vegetables
das	**Getränk, -e**	drink
das	**Glas, ˍ̈er**	glass
das	**Graubrot, -e**	brown bread
das	**Gulasch**	goulash
das	**Kalbfleisch**	veal
das	**Kotelett, -e**	chop
das	**Menü, -s**	menu
das	**Messer**	knife
das	**Mineralwasser**	mineral water
das	**Mittagessen**	lunch; dinner
das	**Obst**	fruit
das	**Öl**	oil
das	**Omelett, -s**	omelette
das	**Picknick, -s** *or* **-e**	picnic
das	**Pils**	lager
die	**Pommes frites** *(pl)*	chips, French fries
das	**Restaurant, -s**	restaurant
das	**Rindfleisch**	beef
das	**Rührei**	scrambled egg

ESSENTIAL WORDS *(feminine continued)*

die	**Teekanne, -n**	teapot
die	**Torte, -n**	flan, tart, cake
die	**Untertasse, -n**	saucer
die	**Wurst, ̈-e**	sausage
die	**Zigarette, -n**	cigarette
die	**Zigarre, -n**	cigar

ESSENTIAL WORDS *(neuter continued)*

das	**Salz**	salt
das	**Schnitzel**	(veal) cutlet
das	**Schwarzbrot**	rye bread
das	**Schweinefleisch**	pork
das	**Spiegelei, -er**	fried egg
das	**Steak, -s**	steak
das	**Wasser**	water
das	**Weißbrot, -e**	white bread
das	**Wiener Schnitzel**	Wiener schnitzel
das	**Wirtshaus, -häuser**	inn
das	**Würstchen**	frankfurter

USEFUL PHRASES

das schmeckt sehr gut **this tastes very nice**
prost! **cheers!**
mit jdm anstoßen **to clink glasses with sb**
süß **sweet**; salzig **salty**; sauer **sour**

IMPORTANT WORDS (masculine)

der	Aschenbecher	ashtray
der	Champagner	champagne
der	Dessertlöffel	dessert spoon
der	Döner	kebab
der	Einkaufswagen	shopping trolley
der	Esslöffel	tablespoon
der	Geschmack, ⁝e	taste
der	Hamburger	hamburger
der	Kaugummi, -s	chewing gum
der	Knoblauch	garlic
der	Knödel	dumpling
der	Kognak, -s	brandy
der	Korken	cork
der	Rinderbraten	roast beef
der	Schnaps, ⁝e	schnapps; spirits
der	Sekt, -e	champagne
der	Stammtisch, -e	*table for the regulars*
der	Strohhalm, -e	(drinking) straw
der	Tabak	tobacco
der	Teelöffel	teaspoon
der	Toast, -s	toast
der	Whisky, -s	whisky

USEFUL PHRASES

rauchen to smoke
danke, ich rauche nicht no thanks, I don't smoke
„Rauchen verboten" "no smoking"
um Feuer bitten to ask for a light
anzünden to light up
ich versuche, das Rauchen aufzugeben I'm trying to give up smoking

IMPORTANT WORDS *(feminine)*

die	**Auswahl (an** + *dat*)	choice (of)
die	**Gaststätte, -n**	restaurant; pub
die	**Getränkekarte, -n**	wine list
die	**Kneipe, -n**	pub
die	**Krabben** *(pl)*	shrimps; prawns
die	**Marmelade, -n**	jam
die	**Mayonnaise, -n**	mayonnaise
die	**Meeresfrüchte** *(pl)*	seafood, shellfish
die	**Nudeln** *(pl)*	pasta, noodles
die	**Orangenmarmelade, -n**	marmalade
die	**Salami, -s**	salami
die	**Salatsoße, -n**	salad dressing
die	**Schale, -n**	bowl
die	**Scheibe, -n**	slice
die	**Schüssel, -n**	bowl, dish
die	**Theke, -n**	bar; counter
die	**Vanillesoße, -n**	custard
die	**Vorspeise, -n**	hors d'œuvre, starter
die	**Weinkarte, -n**	wine list
die	**Wirtschaft, -en**	pub

IMPORTANT WORDS *(neuter)*

das	**Geflügel**	poultry
das	**Gericht, -e**	dish, course
das	**Geschirr**	dishes, crockery
das	**Hauptgericht, -e**	main course
das	**Lammfleisch**	lamb
das	**Mus**	purée
das	**Rezept, -e**	recipe
das	**Sandwich, -es**	sandwich
das	**Tablett, -e**	tray
das	**Trinkgeld, -er**	tip

USEFUL PHRASES

bestellen to order
was können Sie mir empfehlen? what do you recommend?

USEFUL WORDS (masculine)

der	**Eiswürfel**	ice cube
der	**Kaffeefilter**	coffee-maker
der	**Kamillentee**	camomile tea
der	**Kartoffelbrei**	mashed potatoes (pl)
der	**Kartoffelsalat**	potato salad
der	**Krug (¨e) Wasser**	jug of water
der	**Pfannkuchen**	pancake
der	**Pudding**	blancmange
der	**Rahm**	cream
der	**Rotwein**	red wine
der	**(Schinken)speck**	bacon
der	**Teebeutel**	tea bag
der	**Wackelpeter**	jelly
der	**Weinbrand, ¨e**	brandy
der	**Weißwein**	white wine
der	**Zwieback**	toast (in packets)

USEFUL WORDS (feminine)

die	**Büchse, -n**	tin, can
die	**Eisdiele, -n**	ice cream parlour
die	**Frikadelle, -n**	rissole
die	**Konserven (pl)**	preserved foods
die	**Niere, -n**	kidney
die	**Pfeife, -n**	pipe
die	**Serviette, -n**	napkin, serviette
die	**Thermosflasche, -n**	flask

USEFUL WORDS (neuter)

das	**Besteck**	cutlery
das	**Geflügel**	poultry
das	**Kartoffelpüree**	mashed potatoes
das	**Mehl, -e**	flour
das	**Streichholz, ¨er**	match
das	**Tischtuch, ¨er**	tablecloth
das	**Wild**	game (meat)

ESSENTIAL WORDS *(masculine)*

der	Ausflug, ¨e	outing, trip
der	Besuch, -e	visit; visitor
der	Brieffreund, -e	penfriend
der	Computer	computer
der	Fan, -s	fan
der	Film, -e	film
der	(Foto)apparat, -e	camera
der	Freund, -e	friend; boyfriend
der	Jugendklub, -s	youth club
der	MP3-Spieler	MP3 player
der	Plattenspieler	record player
der	Sänger	singer
der	Schlager	hit (record)
der	Spaziergang, ¨e	walk
der	Sport	sport
der	Tanz, ¨e	dance
der	Verein, -e	club

ESSENTIAL WORDS *(feminine)*

die	Brieffreundin	penfriend
die	CD, -s	CD
die	Diskothek, -en	disco
die	DVD, -s	DVD
die	Einladung, -en	invitation
die	Eintrittskarte, -n	(admission) ticket
die	Fotografie, -n	photograph; photography
die	Freizeit	free time, spare time
die	Freundin	friend; girlfriend
die	Musik	music
die	Sängerin	singer
die	Spielkonsole, -n	games console
die	(Spiel)karte, -n	(playing) card
die	Stereoanlage, -en	stereo (system)
die	Zeitschrift, -en	magazine
die	Zeitung, -en	newspaper

ESSENTIAL WORDS *(neuter)*

das	Fernsehen	watching television
das	Fitnessstudio, -s	fitness centre
das	Foto, -s	photograph
das	Hobby, -s	hobby
das	Interesse, -n	interest
das	Kartenspiel, -e	game of cards; pack of cards
das	Kino, -s	cinema
das	Kofferradio, -s	transistor (radio)
das	Konzert, -e	concert
das	Lesen	reading
das	Magazin, -e	magazine
das	Museum, Museen	museum
das	Programm, -e	(TV) programme
das	Radio, -s	radio
das	Singen	singing
das	Spiel, -e	game
das	Taschengeld	pocket money
das	Theater	theatre
das	Wandern	hiking, rambling
das	Wochenende, -n	weekend

USEFUL PHRASES

in meiner Freizeit **in my free or spare time**
die Zeit damit verbringen, etw zu tun **to spend time doing sth**
am Wochenende **at the weekend(s)**
sich ausruhen **to rest**; beschließen **to decide**; treffen **to meet**
viel Spaß! **enjoy yourself!, have fun!**
es hat mir wirklich gut gefallen **I really liked it**
ausgezeichnet! **excellent!**; toll! **terrific!**
einen Spaziergang machen **to go for a walk**
fernsehen **to watch television**
Radio hören **to listen to the radio**
umschalten **to turn over, change channels**
CDs hören **to play CDs**; aufnehmen **to record**
fotografieren **to take photos (of)**; knipsen **to snap**
lesen **to read**; schreiben **to write**; sammeln **to collect**
malen **to paint**; zeichnen **to draw**

IMPORTANT WORDS (masculine)

der	Drachen	kite; hang-glider
der	Karneval, -e or -s	carnival
der	Krimi, -s	thriller, detective story
der	Pfadfinder	boy scout
der	Roman, -e	novel
der	Shoppingsender	shopping channel
der	Treffpunkt, -e	meeting place
der	Videorekorder	video (recorder)
der	Walkman®	personal stereo, Walkman®
der	Zoo, -s	zoo

IMPORTANT WORDS (feminine)

die	Aufnahme, -n	shot (photo); recording
die	Ausstellung, -en	exhibition
die	Besichtigung, -en	visit
die	(Briefmarken)sammlung, -en	(stamp) collection
die	Disko, -s	disco
die	Freizeitbeschäftigung, -en	hobby, spare-time activity
die	Illustrierte, -n	magazine
die	Musikkassette, -n	music cassette
die	Nachrichten (pl)	news, newscast
die	Pfadfinderin	girl scout
die	Sendung, -en	transmission, programme
die	Spielshow, -s	game show
die	Unterhaltung, -en	entertainment; talk
die	Verabredung, -en	date, appointment
die	Videokassette, -n	video (cassette)
die	Wanderung, -en	walk, hike

IMPORTANT WORDS (neuter)

das	Dia, -s	slide, transparency
das	Mitglied, -er	member
das	Schach	chess
das	Taschenbuch, ¨er	paperback

USEFUL WORDS (masculine)

der	CD-Spieler	CD player
das	Chatraum, -räume	chatroom
die	Comics (pl)	cartoons, comic strips
der	Feierabend, -e	end of work, evening
der	Ohrstöpsel	earplug
der	Spielautomat, -en	slot machine
der	Zeitvertreib, -e	pastime

USEFUL WORDS (feminine)

die	CD, -s, die Compact Disc, - -s	compact disc, CD
die	Fernsehsendung, -en	TV programme
die	Filmkamera, -s	cine camera
die	Freizeitdroge, -n	recreational drug
die	Hitliste, -n	charts, top twenty
die	Hitparade, -en	charts, hit parade
die	Party, -s	party
die	Versammlung, -en	meeting, gathering

USEFUL WORDS (neuter)

das	Album, Alben	album
das	Damespiel	draughts
das	Feriendorf, ¨-er	holiday camp
das	Ferienlager	school camp
das	Freizeitzentrum, -zentren	leisure centre
das	Gleitschirmfliegen	paragliding
das	Jugendzentrum, -zentren	youth centre
das	Kegeln	bowling
das	Kreuzworträtsel	crossword (puzzle)
das	Lied, -er	song
das	Skateboard, -s	skateboard
das	Snowboard, -s	snowboard
das	Surfen	surfing

USEFUL PHRASES

ich interessiere mich für (+ acc) I am interested in ...
eine Party geben to have a party
hast du Lust, zu meiner Party zu kommen? do you fancy coming to my party?

ESSENTIAL + IMPORTANT WORDS (*masculine*)

der Apfel, ⁝	apple
der Apfelbaum, -bäume	apple tree
der Birnbaum, -bäume	pear tree
der Obstbaum, -bäume	fruit tree
der Obstgarten, ⁝	orchard
der Pfirsich, -e	peach
der Pfirsichbaum, -bäume	peach tree
der Weinstock, ⁝e	vine

ESSENTIAL + IMPORTANT WORDS (*feminine*)

die Apfelsine, -n	orange
die Banane, -n	banana; banana tree
die Birne, -n	pear
die Erdbeere, -n	strawberry
eine Frucht, ⁝e	a (*piece of*) fruit
die Himbeere, -n	raspberry
die Kirsche, -n	cherry
die Melone, -n	melon
die Olive, -n	olive
die Orange, -n	orange; orange tree
die Pflaume, -n	plum
die Schale, -n	skin; peel; shell
die (Wein)traube, -n	grape; bunch of grapes
die Zitrone, -n	lemon

ESSENTIAL WORDS (*neuter*)

das Kompott, -e	stewed fruit
das Obst	fruit
das Stück Obst	piece of fruit

USEFUL PHRASES

reif ripe; unreif not ripe; süß sweet; bitter sour, bitter
hart hard; weich soft; saftig juicy
pflücken to pick; sammeln to gather
essen to eat; beißen to bite
blaue/grüne Trauben black/green grapes

USEFUL WORDS (masculine)

der Granatapfel, ⁻	pomegranate
der Kern, -e	pip, stone (in fruit)
der Nussbaum, -bäume	walnut tree
der Rhabarber	rhubarb
der Walnussbaum, -bäume	walnut tree
der Weinberg, -e	vineyard
der Weinstock, ⁻e	vine

USEFUL WORDS (feminine)

die Ananas, - or -se	pineapple
die Aprikose, -n	apricot; apricot tree
die Backpflaume, -n	prune
die Beere, -n	berry
die Brombeere, -n	blackberry, bramble
die Dattel, -n	date
die Erdnuss, ⁻e	peanut
die Feige, -n	fig
die Grapefruit	grapefruit
die Haselnuss, ⁻e	hazelnut
die Heidelbeere, -n	bilberry
die Johannisbeere, -n	redcurrant
die Schwarze Johannisbeere, -n -n	blackcurrant
die Kastanie, -n	chestnut; chestnut tree
die Kiwi, -s	kiwi (fruit)
die Kokosnuss, ⁻e	coconut
die Mandarine, -n	tangerine
die Nuss, ⁻e	nut
die Pampelmuse, -n	grapefruit
die Passionsfrucht, ⁻e	passion fruit
die Stachelbeere, -n	gooseberry
die Traube, -n	grape; bunch of grapes
die Traubenlese	grape harvest, vintage
die Walnuss, ⁻e	walnut
die (Wein)rebe, -n	vine
die Zwetsch(g)e, -n	plum

ESSENTIAL WORDS (*masculine*)

der **Fernsehapparat, -e** *or* der **Fernseher**	television set
der **Herd, -e**	cooker
der **Kleiderschrank, ⁻e**	wardrobe
der **Kühlschrank, ⁻e**	fridge, refrigerator
der **Plattenspieler**	record player
der **Raum, Räume**	room
der **Satellitenempfänger**	satellite receiver
der **Schrank, ⁻e**	cupboard
der **Sessel**	armchair
der **Stuhl, ⁻e**	chair
der **Tisch, -e**	table
der **Wecker**	alarm clock

ESSENTIAL WORDS (*feminine*)

die **Lampe, -n**	lamp
die **Stehlampe, -n**	standard lamp, floor lamp
die **Stereoanlage, -n**	stereo system
die **Uhr, -en**	clock
die **Waschmaschine, -n**	washing machine

ESSENTIAL WORDS (*neuter*)

das **Bett, -en**	bed
das **Bild, -er**	picture, painting
das **Haus, Häuser**	house
das **Sofa, -s**	settee, couch
das **Telefon, -e**	telephone
das **Zimmer**	room

USEFUL PHRASES
fernsehen to watch television; im Fernsehen on television
telefonieren to telephone; anrufen to phone, call
Musik hören to listen to music
programmieren to program

IMPORTANT WORDS *(masculine)*

der **CD-Brenner**	CD burner
der **CD-Spieler**	CD player
der **DVD-Brenner**	DVD burner
der **DVD-Spieler**	DVD player
der **Elektroherd, -e**	electric cooker
der **Gasherd, -e**	gas cooker
der **Nachttisch, -e**	bedside table
der **Ofen, ̈**	oven
der **Spiegel**	mirror
der **Videorekorder**	video recorder

IMPORTANT WORDS *(feminine)*

die **Digicam, -s**	digicam
die **Schreibmaschine, -n**	typewriter
die **Spülmaschine, -n**	dishwasher
die **Steckdose, -n**	(wall) socket

IMPORTANT WORDS *(neuter)*

das **(Bücher)regal, -e**	bookcase, bookshelves
ein **digitales Radio, -n -s**	digital radio
das **Fax, -e**	fax
das **Handy, -s**	mobile phone
die **Möbel** *(pl)*	furniture
das **Möbel(stück)**	piece of furniture
das **Regal, -e**	(set of) shelves
das **Videogerät, -e**	video (recorder)
das **Walkman**®	personal stereo, Walkman®

USEFUL PHRASES

ein Zimmer möblieren to furnish a room
ein möbliertes Zimmer a furnished room
bequem comfortable; unbequem uncomfortable
in dem Zimmer ist es sehr eng the room is very cramped
den Tisch decken/abräumen to lay *or* set/to clear the table
das Bett machen to make the bed
ins Bett gehen, zu Bett gehen to go to bed

USEFUL WORDS *(masculine)*

der	Anrufbeantworter	answering machine
der	Backofen, ⸚	oven
der	Beamer	data projector
der	Bücherschrank, ⸚e	bookcase
der	Couchtisch, -e	coffee table
der	Esstisch, -e	dining table
der	Frisiertisch, -e	dressing table
der	Heizofen, ⸚	fire, heater
der	Hocker	stool
der	Kabelanschluss, ⸚e	cable connection
der	Lehnsessel *or* der Lehnstuhl, ⸚e	armchair
der	Mikrowellenherd, -e	microwave oven
der	Möbelwagen	furniture van, removal van
der	Nachtspeicherofen	(night-)storage heater
der	Radiowecker	radio alarm clock
der	Satz (⸚e) Tische	nest of tables
der	Schaukelstuhl, ⸚e	rocking chair
der	Schirmständer	umbrella stand
der	Schnellkochtopf, ⸚e	pressure cooker
der	Schreibtisch, -e	writing desk
der	Sekretär, -e	bureau, writing desk
der	Staubsauger	vacuum cleaner, Hoover®
der	Teewagen	trolley
der	Umluftherd, -e	fan-assisted oven
der	Umzug, ⸚e	removal
der	Wäschetrockner	tumble dryer

USEFUL PHRASES

sitzen to sit, be sitting; sich setzen to sit down
sich hinlegen to lie down; sich ausruhen to rest
ein Zimmer ausräumen to clear out a room
ein Zimmer aufräumen *or* in Ordnung bringen to tidy up a room
putzen to clean; abstauben to dust; staubsaugen to hoover

USEFUL WORDS (feminine)

die	Anrichte, -n	dresser; sideboard
die	Antenne, -n	aerial
die	Einrichtung	furnishings (pl)
die	Fernbedienung, -en	remote control
die	Gefriertruhe, -n	freezer
die	Kommode, -n	chest of drawers
die	Matratze, -n	mattress
die	Nähmaschine, -n	sewing machine
die	Satellitenantenne, -n	satellite dish
die	Schublade, -n	drawer
die	Spedition, -en	removal firm
die	Standuhr, -en	grandfather clock
die	Tiefkühltruhe, -n	freezer, deep freeze
die	Truhe, -n	chest, trunk
die	Videokamera, -s	video camera
die	Wäscheschleuder, -n	spin dryer
die	Waage, -n	(bathroom) scales
die	Wiege, -n	cradle

USEFUL WORDS (neuter)

das	Bord, -e	shelf
das	Etagenbett, -en	bunk bed
das	Gemälde	painting, picture
das	Gerät, -e	appliance
das	Kinderbettchen	cot
das	Rollo, -s or das Rouleau, -s	blind
das	Schubfach, ¨er	drawer
ein	schnurlose Telefon, -n -e	cordless telephone
das	Tonbandgerät, -e	tape recorder

USEFUL PHRASES

elektrisch electric; anmachen, einschalten to turn or switch on
ausmachen, ausschalten to turn or switch off
es funktioniert nicht it's not working
heizen to heat; gemütlich comfortable, cosy

die	**Alpen** *(pl)*	the Alps
	Antwerpen *(nt)*	Antwerp
der	**Ärmelkanal**	the English Channel
der	**Atlantik,**	the Atlantic (Ocean)
der	**Atlantische Ozean**	
	Basel *(nt)*	Basle
	Bayern *(nt)*	Bavaria
	Berlin *(nt)*	Berlin
der	**Bodensee**	Lake Constance
die	**Britischen Inseln** *(fpl)*	the British Isles
	Brüssel *(nt)*	Brussels
die	**Donau**	the Danube
	Edinburg *(nt)*	Edinburgh
die	**Elbe**	the (river) Elbe
das	**Elsass** *(nt)*	Alsace
der	**Ferne Osten**	the Far East
	Genf *(nt)*	Geneva
der	**Genfer See**	Lake Geneva
	Gent *(nt)*	Ghent
Den	**Haag** *(nt)*	The Hague
	Hannover *(nt)*	Hanover
	Kairo *(nt)*	Cairo
die	**Kanalinseln** *(fpl)*	the Channel Islands
	Köln *(nt)*	Cologne
	Korsika *(nt)*	Corsica
	Lissabon *(nt)*	Lisbon
	Lothringen *(nt)*	Lorraine
	Mailand *(nt)*	Milan
	Mallorca *(nt)*	Majorca
das	**Mittelmeer**	the Mediterranean
die	**Mosel**	Moselle
	Moskau *(nt)*	Moscow
	München *(nt)*	Munich
der	**Nahe Osten**	the Middle East
die	**Nordsee**	the North Sea
die	**Ostsee**	the Baltic Sea
der	**Pazifik,**	the Pacific (Ocean)
der	**Pazifische Ozean**	
	Peking *(nt)*	Beijing
die	**Pyrenäen** *(pl)*	the Pyrenees

der	**Rhein**	the Rhine
	Rom *(nt)*	Rome
der	**Schwarzwald**	the Black Forest
die	**Seine**	the Seine
der	**Stille Ozean**	the Pacific Ocean
die	**Themse**	the Thames
	Venedig *(nt)*	Venice
der	**Vesuv**	Mount Vesuvius
	Warschau *(nt)*	Warsaw
	Wien *(nt)*	Vienna
die	**Wolga**	the Volga

USEFUL PHRASES

Athener, -in an Athenian
Bas(e)ler, -in a person from Basle
Bayer, -in a Bavarian
Böhme, Böhmin a person from Bohemia
Elsässer, -in a person from Alsace, an Alsatian
Flame, Flamin *or* Flämin a person from Flanders, a Fleming
Friese, Friesin a person from Frisia, a Frisian
Hamburger, -in a person from Hamburg
Hannoveraner, -in a person from Hanover, a Hanoverian
Hesse, Hessin a person from Hesse
Indianer, -in an (American) Indian
Londoner, -in a Londoner
Moskauer, -in a person from Moscow, a Muscovite
Münch(e)ner, -in a person from Munich
Neapolitaner, -in a Neapolitan
Pariser, -in a Parisian
Preuße, Preußin a Prussian
Rheinländer, -in a Rheinlander
Römer, -in a person from Rome, a Roman
Sachse, Sächsin a person from Saxony
Schwabe, Schwäbin a person from Swabia
Tiroler, -in a person from the Tyrol
Venezianer, -in a Venetian
Westfale, Westfälin a Westphalian
Wiener, -in a person from Vienna, a Viennese

GREETINGS AND FAREWELLS

guten Tag! good day, hello; good afternoon
guten Morgen! good morning
guten Abend! good evening
gute Nacht! good night *(when going to bed)*
auf Wiedersehen! goodbye
auf Wiederhören! goodbye *(on phone)*
hallo! hi!; **tschüss!** bye!; **servus** hello; goodbye
grüß Gott! hello
wie geht's?; **wie geht es Ihnen?** how are things?
gut, danke; **es geht mir gut, danke** very well, thank you
sehr angenehm pleased to meet you
bis später see you later
bis morgen see you tomorrow

BEST WISHES

ich gratuliere! congratulations!
alles Gute all the best, best wishes
herzlichen Glückwunsch congratulations, best wishes
alles Gute zum Geburtstag happy birthday
alles Gute zum Hochzeitstag congratulations on your wedding day
viel Glück all the best; the best of luck
machs gut! take care
fröhliche Weihnachten merry Christmas
gutes neues Jahr happy New Year
guten Appetit! have a good meal, enjoy your meal
prost! cheers; **zum Wohl!** good health!
Gesundheit! bless you! *(after a sneeze)*
viel Spaß! have a good time, enjoy yourself *etc*
schlaf gut! sleep well
gut geschlafen? did you sleep well?

grüßen, begrüßen to greet, welcome
sich verabschieden to say goodbye, take one's leave
(sich) vorstellen to introduce (oneself)

SURPRISE

ach du meine Güte oh my goodness, oh dear
so?, wirklich? really?
so, so! well, well!; ach so! oh I see!
na, so etwas! you don't say!
wie? what?
was für ein Glück! what a piece of luck!

POLITENESS

bitte please, excuse me
danke thank you; nein danke no thank you
ja bitte, bitte ja yes please
tu das ja nicht don't do that
danke schön, danke sehr, vielen Dank thank you very much, many thanks
nichts zu danken don't mention it
bitte schön, bitte sehr don't mention it
gern geschehen my pleasure, don't mention it
entschuldigen Sie, Entschuldigung excuse me, I'm sorry
verzeihen Sie, Verzeihung I'm sorry, I beg your pardon
pardon excuse me, I'm sorry
das macht nichts it doesn't matter
(wie) bitte? (I beg your) pardon?
hier bitte, bitte schön, bitte sehr there you are
mit Vergnügen with pleasure
machen Sie keine Umstände don't go to any trouble

WARNINGS

Achtung! watch out!; Vorsicht! be careful!
pass auf! look out!, watch out!
halten Sie! stop!
Feuer! fire!; haltet den Dieb! stop thief!
Ruhe!, ruhig! be quiet!; halt den Mund! shut up!
herein! come in!; hinaus! get out!
beeile dich! hurry up!; hau ab! clear off!
geh mir aus dem Weg! get out of my way!

AGREEMENT AND DISAGREEMENT

ja yes; **doch** yes *(when contradictory)*
nein no
jawohl yes indeed
natürlich of course
natürlich nicht, aber nein of course not
nicht wahr? isn't that right?
in Ordnung O.K., all right
gut good, O.K.
na gut, also gut O.K. then, all right then
schön fine
einverstanden! agreed!
genau, ganz recht exactly
desto besser so much the better
ich habe nichts dagegen I don't mind *or* object
das ist mir gleich *or* **einerlei** *or* **egal** I don't mind, it's all the same to me, it's all one to me
das stimmt that's right
das stimmt nicht that doesn't make sense
im Gegenteil on the contrary
nie!, um nichts in der Welt! never!, not on your life!
kümmern Sie sich um Ihre eigenen Dinge! mind your own business!
nieder mit ... down with ...

DISTRESS

Hilfe! help!
ach je! oh dear!
ach!, o weh! alas!
was ist los (mit dir)? what's the matter (with you)?, what's wrong (with you)?
leider (nicht) unfortunately (not)
es tut mir leid I'm sorry
es tut mir wirklich leid I'm really sorry
wie schade what a pity
das ist Pech it's a shame, that's bad luck
verflixt (noch mal)! blow!, drat!, dash it!
verflucht!, verdammt! damn!
ich habe es satt I'm fed up with it
ich kann ihn nicht ausstehen I can't stand him
was soll ich tun? what shall I do?
wie ärgerlich! what a nuisance!, how annoying!

OTHER EXPRESSIONS

vielleicht perhaps, maybe
ich weiß nicht I don't know
(ich habe) keine Ahnung (I've) no idea
ich weiß da nicht Bescheid I don't know (anything about it)
ich weiß nicht genau I don't know exactly
das kann ich mir vorstellen I can believe that
schade! shame!
mein Gott! good Lord!
(ach) du lieber Himmel! (good) heavens!, goodness gracious!
prima! great!
klasse! terrific!, marvellous!
machen Sie sich keine Sorgen don't worry
aber wirklich! well really!
du machst wohl Witze you must be joking or kidding!
so eine Frechheit! what a nerve or cheek!
armes Ding! poor thing!

ESSENTIAL WORDS (masculine)

der	Arzt, ⁝e	doctor, G.P.
der	Durchfall	diarrhoea
die	Kopfschmerzen (pl)	a headache
	Kranke(r), -n	patient
der	Krankenwagen	ambulance
der	Zahnarzt, ⁝e	dentist

ESSENTIAL WORDS (feminine)

die	Allergie, -n	allergy
die	Ärztin	doctor, G.P.
die	Erkältung, -en	cold; chill
die	erste Hilfe	first aid
die	Gesundheit	health
die	Grippe	flu, influenza
die	Klinik, -en	hospital, clinic
die	Krankenschwester, -n	nurse
die	Krankheit, -en	illness
die	Lebensgefahr	danger (to life)
die	Medizin	(science of) medicine
die	Pille, -n	pill
die	Tablette, -n	tablet, pill
die	Temperatur, -en	temperature
die	Verstopfung, -en	constipation

ESSENTIAL WORDS (neuter)

das	Fieber	fever, (high) temperature
das	Heimweh	homesickness
das	Kopfweh	headache
das	Krankenhaus, -häuser	hospital

USEFUL PHRASES

krank ill; gesund healthy; wohl well
schwach weak; atemlos breathless
müde tired; schwindlig dizzy; blass pale
sich erkälten to catch cold; erkältet sein to have a cold
husten to cough; niesen to sneeze; schwitzen to sweat

IMPORTANT WORDS (masculine)

der	Apotheker	(dispensing) chemist
der	Atem	breath
der	Auslandskrankenschein, -e	(European) health insurance card
die	Bauchschmerzen (pl)	stomach-ache
der	Gips	plaster; plaster of Paris
die	Halsschmerzen (pl)	a sore throat
der	Husten	cough
der	Krankenpfleger	(male) nurse
der	Krankenschein, -e	health insurance card
der	Krebs	cancer
die	Magenschmerzen (pl)	stomach-ache
der	Operationssaal, -säle	operating theatre
der	Patient, -en	patient
der	Schmerz, -en	pain, ache
der	Schnupfen	cold (in the head)
der	Schweiß	sweat
der	Sonnenbrand, ⁻e	sunburn
der	Tod, -e	death
der	Tropfen	drop
der	Verband, ⁻e	bandage, dressing
die	Zahnschmerzen (pl)	toothache

IMPORTANT WORDS (feminine)

die	Behandlung	treatment
die	Feuerwehr, -en	fire brigade
die	Krankenkasse, -n	health insurance
die	Kur, -en	health cure
die	Operation, -en	operation
die	Patientin	patient
die	Ruhe	rest
die	Sorge, -n	care, worry
die	Spritze, -n	syringe; injection
die	Untersuchung, -en	medical examination
die	Verletzung, -en	injury
die	Versichertenkarte, -n	health insurance card
die	Wunde, -n	wound

IMPORTANT WORDS (neuter)

das	**Aids**	AIDS, aids
das	**Aspirin**	aspirin
das	**Blut**	blood
das	**Heftpflaster**	sticking plaster
das	**Kondom, -e**	condom
das	**Medikament, -e**	medicine
das	**Rezept, -e**	prescription
das	**Thermometer**	thermometer
das	**Verhütungsmittel**	contraceptive

USEFUL WORDS (feminine)

die	**Abmagerungskur, -en**	(slimming) diet
die	**Akne**	acne
die	**Blase, -n**	blister; bladder
die	**Blinddarmentzündung, -en**	appendicitis
die	**Blutübertragung, -en**	blood transfusion
die	**Chemotherapie, -n**	chemotherapy
die	**Diät, -en**	(special) diet
die	**Droge, -n**	drug
die	**Epidemie, -n**	epidemic
die	**Genesung**	recovery
die	**Kraft, ⁻e**	strength, power
die	**Magenverstimmung**	stomach upset
die	**Mandelentzündung**	tonsillitis
die	**Masern** (pl)	measles
die	**Migräne**	migraine
die	**Narbe, -n**	scar
die	**Poliklinik, -en**	health centre
die	**Röntgenaufnahme, -n**	X-ray
die	**Röteln** (pl)	German measles
die	**Salbe, -n**	ointment, cream
die	**Schwangerschaft, -en**	pregnancy
die	**Station, -en**	ward
die	**Übelkeit**	sickness, vomiting
die	**Watte**	cotton wool
die	**Windpocken** (pl)	chickenpox

USEFUL WORDS (masculine)

der	Bazillus, Bazillen	germ
der	blaue Fleck, -n -en	bruise
der	Blutdruck	blood pressure
der	Drogenmissbrauch	drug abuse
der	Fußpilz	athlete's foot
der	Heuschnupfen	hayfever
	HIV-Infizierte(r), -n	person who is HIV-positive
der	Kratzer	scratch
der	Mumps	mumps
der	Puls	pulse
der	Rollstuhl, ̈-e	wheelchair
der	Schlaganfall, ̈-e	stroke
der	Schock, -s	shock
der	Sonnenstich, -e	sunstroke
der	Stress	stress
der	Stich, -e	sting

USEFUL WORDS (neuter)

das	Altersheim, -e	old people's home
das	Antibiotikum, -ka	antibiotic
das	Gift, -e	poison
das	Rauschgift, -e	drug, narcotic
das	Sprechzimmer	surgery, consulting room
das	Wartezimmer	waiting room

USEFUL PHRASES

fallen, stürzen to fall; brechen to break
ich bin mit dem Auto verunglückt I've had an accident with the car
was fehlt Ihnen? what's the matter with you?
es blutet it's bleeding; es tut weh it hurts
verletzt injured, hurt; verwundet wounded
sich übergeben to vomit, be sick
untersuchen to examine; verbinden to bandage
pflegen to look after, nurse; behandeln to treat
verschreiben to prescribe; gute Besserung! get well soon!
sich erholen to recover; sterben to die; tot dead

ESSENTIAL WORDS *(masculine)*

der **(Farb)fernseher**	(colour) television set
der **Gast, ¨e**	guest
der **Gasthof, ¨e**	hotel, inn
der **Kellner**	waiter
der **Koch, ¨e**	cook
der **Koffer**	case, suitcase
der **Lift, -e** *or* **-s**	lift
der **Notausgang, ¨e**	emergency exit
der **Reisepass, ¨e**	passport
der **Schalter**	switch
der **Scheck, -s**	cheque
der **Schlüssel**	key
der **Stock, Stockwerke**	floor, storey
der **Tag, -e**	day
der **Weinkellner**	wine waiter
der **Zuschlag, ¨e**	extra charge

ESSENTIAL WORDS *(feminine)*

die **Anmeldung**	registration
die **Antwort, -en**	answer
die **Bar, -s**	bar
die **Bedienung**	service; service charge
die **Dusche, -n**	shower
die **Halbpension**	half board
die **Kellnerin**	waitress
die **Köchin**	cook
die **Mahlzeit, -en**	meal
die **Nacht, ¨e**	night
die **Pension, -en**	guest-house, boarding house
die **Rechnung, -en**	bill
die **Tasche, -n**	bag
die **Toilette, -n**	toilet
die **Übernachtung mit Frühstück**	bed and breakfast
die **Vollpension**	full board
die **Woche, -n**	week

ESSENTIAL + IMPORTANT WORDS *(neuter)*

das	Badezimmer	bathroom
das	Café, -s	café
das	Doppelbett, -en	double bed
das	Doppelzimmer	double room
das	Einzelzimmer	single room
das	Erdgeschoss, -e	ground floor, ground level
das	(Farb)fernsehen	(colour) television
das	Formular, -e	form
das	Freibad, ⁻er	open-air swimming pool
das	Fremdenzimmer	guest room
das	Frühstück, -e	breakfast
das	Gasthaus, -häuser	inn, hotel
das	Gepäck	luggage
das	Hotel, -s	hotel
das	Kleingeld	small change
das	Mittagessen	lunch
das	Restaurant, -s	restaurant
das	Speisezimmer	dining room
das	(Tele)fax, -e	fax
das	Telefon, -e	telephone
das	Treppenhaus, -häuser	staircase
das	Wirtshaus, -häuser	inn
das	Zimmer	room
das	Zimmermädchen	chambermaid

USEFUL PHRASES

einpacken to get packed; auspacken to get unpacked
ich habe schon gebucht I have already booked
eine Reservierung bestätigen to confirm a reservation
sich in einem Hotel anmelden to book in at a hotel
ich möchte hier übernachten I'd like a room for the night here
ein Formular ausfüllen to fill in a form
3 Tage bleiben to stay for 3 days

IMPORTANT WORDS (masculine)

der	Aufenthalt, -e	stay
der	Aufzug, -̈e	lift
der	Balkon, -s or -e	balcony
der	Blick, -e	view
der	Empfangschef, -s	receptionist, reception clerk
der	Feuerlöscher	fire extinguisher
der	Gepäckträger	porter
der	Hotelier, -s	hotelier, hotel-keeper
der	Prospekt, -e	leaflet, brochure
der	Reiseführer	guide-book; travel guide (person)
der	Reiseleiter	travel courier
der	Stern, -e	star

IMPORTANT WORDS (feminine)

die	Aussicht, -en	view
die	Empfangsdame, -n	receptionist
die	Garderobe, -n	cloakroom
die	Gaststätte, -n	restaurant; pub
die	Kneipe, -n	pub
die	Mehrwertsteuer	value added tax
die	Nummer, -n	number
die	Rezeption, -en	reception, reception desk
die	Terrasse, -n	terrace
die	Unterkunft, -künfte	accommodation
die	Veranstaltung, -en	organization

USEFUL WORDS (*masculine*)

der	**Brand, ⁻e**	fire
der	**(Gast)wirt, -e**	owner, innkeeper, landlord
der	**Ober**	waiter
der	**Oberkellner**	head waiter

USEFUL WORDS (*feminine*)

die	**(Gast)wirtin**	owner, innkeeper, landlady
die	**Vorhalle, -n**	foyer

USEFUL WORDS (*neuter*)

das	**Foyer**	foyer
das	**Kellergeschoss, -e**	basement
das	**Schwimmbecken**	swimming pool
das	**Stockwerk, -e**	floor, storey
das	**Trinkgeld, -er**	tip
das	**Wechselgeld**	change
das	**Zweibettzimmer**	twin-bedded room

USEFUL PHRASES

ich möchte ein Zimmer mit Dusche/mit Bad I'd like a room with
   a shower/with a bath

was kostet es?, wie teuer ist es? how much is it?

das ist ziemlich teuer that is rather expensive

das Zimmer hat Aussicht *or* Blick auf den Strand the room overlooks the
   beach

im ersten/zehnten Stock on the first/tenth floor

im Erdgeschoss on the ground floor, on ground level

Herr Ober! waiter!

Fräulein! excuse me, miss!

„Bedienung inbegriffen" "service included"

„inklusive Bedienung" "inclusive of service"

„Sie brauchen nur zu klingeln" "just ring"

„Zimmer frei" "vacancies"

ESSENTIAL WORDS *(masculine)*

der	Bungalow, -s	bungalow
der	Flur, -e	(entrance) hall
der	(Fuß)boden, ⸚	floor
der	Garten, ⸚	garden
der	Haushalt	household
der	Hof, ⸚e	yard
der	Keller	cellar
der	Mieter	tenant
der	Park, -s	public park
der	Parkplatz, ⸚e	parking space
der	Raum, Räume	room; space
der	Schlüssel	key
der	Speisesaal, -säle	dining room
der	Stein, -e	stone
der	Stock, Stockwerke	floor, storey

ESSENTIAL WORDS *(feminine)*

die	Adresse, -n	address
die	Dusche, -n	shower
die	Familie, -n	family
die	Garage, -n	garage
die	Hausfrau, -en	housewife
die	Haustür, -en	front door
die	Küche, -n	kitchen; cooking
die	Miete, -n	rent
die	Stadt, ⸚e	town
die	Straße, -n	street, road
die	Toilette, -n	toilet
die	Treppe, -n	stairs, staircase
die	Tür, -en	door
die	Wand, ⸚e	(inside) wall
die	Wohnung, -en	flat

USEFUL PHRASES

in der Stadt/auf dem Lande wohnen to live in the town/in the country
mieten to rent; bauen to build; besitzen to own

ESSENTIAL WORDS (neuter)

das	Bad, ̈-er; das Badezimmer	bathroom
das	Doppelhaus, -häuser	semi-detached (house)
das	Dorf, ̈-er	village
das	Einfamilienhaus, -häuser	detached house
das	Erdgeschoss, -e	ground floor, ground level
das	Esszimmer	dining room
das	Fenster	window
das	Haus, Häuser	house
das	Klo, das Klosett	toilet, loo
das	Reihenhaus, -häuser	terraced house
das	Schlafzimmer	bedroom
das	Schloss, ̈-er	lock
das	Treppenhaus	staircase
das	Wohnzimmer	lounge, living room
das	Zentrum, Zentren	centre
das	Zimmer	room

IMPORTANT WORDS (neuter)

das	Dach, ̈-er	roof
das	Gebäude	building
das	Gebiet, -e	area
das	Hochhaus, -häuser	high-rise (building)
die	Möbel (pl)	furniture
das	Möbel(stück)	piece of furniture
das	Parkett, -e	wooden or parquet floor
das	Tor, -e	gate

USEFUL WORDS (neuter)

das	Arbeitszimmer	study
das	Dachfenster	skylight
das	Gästezimmer	spare room, guest room
das	Kellergeschoss, -e	basement
das	Oberlicht, -er	skylight
das	Stockwerk, -e	floor, storey

IMPORTANT WORDS *(masculine)*

der **Aufzug, ⁻e**	lift
der **Balkon, -s** *or* **-e**	balcony
der **Bezirk, -e**	district
der **Dachboden, ⁻**	attic, loft
der **Einwohner**	inhabitant
der **Gang, ⁻e**	corridor
der **Kamin, -e**	chimney; fireplace
der **Landkreis, -e**	region
der **Nachbar, -n**	neighbour
der **Rasen**	lawn; grass
der **Vorort, -e**	suburb

IMPORTANT WORDS *(feminine)*

die **Anlage, -n**	layout
die **Aussicht, -en**	view
die **Decke, -n**	ceiling
die **Gegend, -en**	district, area
die **Kohle, -n**	coal
die **Lage, -n**	position, situation
die **Mauer, -n**	*(outside)* wall
die **Nachbarin**	neighbour
die **Telefonnummer, -n**	phone number
die **Terrasse, -n**	patio
die **Türklingel, -n**	doorbell
die **Umgebung, -en**	surroundings *(pl)*
die **Zentralheizung, -en**	central heating

USEFUL PHRASES

es klopft somebody's knocking at the door
es klingelt somebody's ringing the doorbell
im ersten/dritten Stock on the first/third floor
im Erdgeschoss on the ground floor, on ground level
oben upstairs; unten downstairs
zu Hause, daheim at home
umziehen to move (house); einziehen to move in
sich einleben to settle down, settle in

USEFUL WORDS (masculine)

der	Besitzer	owner
der	(Fenster)laden, ⸚e	shutter
der or das	(Fenster)sims, -e	window sill or ledge
der	Hausmeister	caretaker
der	Hauswirt, -e	landlord
der or das	Kaminsims, -e	mantelpiece
der	Korridor, -e	corridor
der	Rauch	smoke
der	Schornstein, -e	chimney
der	(Treppen)absatz, ⸚e	landing
der	Umzug, ⸚e	removal
der	Wintergarten, ⸚	conservatory
der	Wohnblock, -s	block of flats
der	Zaun, Zäune	fence

USEFUL WORDS (feminine)

die	Allee, -n	avenue
die	Antenne, -n	aerial
die	Einrichtung, -en	furnishings (pl)
die	Etagenwohnung, -en	flat
die	Fensterscheibe, -n	window pane
die	Fliese, -n	tile
die	Gasse, -n	lane (in town)
die	Hecke, -n	hedge
die	Jalousie, -n	venetian blind
die	Kachel, -n	(wall) tile
die	Kellerwohnung, -en	basement flat
die	Mansarde, -n	attic
die	Putzfrau, -en	cleaner
die	Rumpelkammer, -n	box room, junk room
die	Stube, -n	room
die	(Tür)stufe, -n	(door)step
die	Verandatür, -en	French window
die	(Wohn)siedlung, -en	housing estate

ESSENTIAL WORDS (masculine)

der	Briefkasten, ⸚	letterbox
der	Fernsehapparat, -e or	television set
	der Fernseher	
der	Föhn, -e	hair-drier
der	Knopf, ⸚e	knob, button
der	Kühlschrank, ⸚e	fridge
der	Schalter	switch
der	Schrank, ⸚e	cupboard
der	Topf, ⸚e	pot
der	Wecker	alarm clock

ESSENTIAL WORDS (feminine)

die	Bürste, -n	brush
die	Dusche, -n	shower
die	Farbe, -n	paint; colour
die	Gardine, -n	curtain
die	Hausarbeit	housework
die	Kanne, -n	jug; pot
die	Lampe, -n	lamp
die	Sachen (pl)	things
die	Seife	soap
die	Zahnbürste, -n	toothbrush
die	Zahncreme, -s or	toothpaste
	die Zahnpasta, -pasten	

ESSENTIAL WORDS (neuter)

das	Bild, -er	picture, painting
das	Handtuch, ⸚er	towel
das	Licht, -er	light
das	Poster	poster
das	Wasser	water

USEFUL PHRASES

die Hausarbeit machen to do the housework
duschen to have a shower; baden to have a bath

IMPORTANT WORDS (masculine)

der	Abfall, ¨e	rubbish, refuse
der	Abfalleimer	rubbish bin
der	Aschenbecher	ashtray
der	Haartrockner	hair-drier
der	Kamm, ¨e	comb
der	Rasierapparat, -e	razor
der	Spiegel	mirror
der	Teppich, -e	carpet
der	Vorhang, ¨e	curtain
der	(Wasser)hahn, ¨e	tap

IMPORTANT WORDS (feminine)

die	(Bade)wanne, -n	bath
die	(Bett)decke, -n	blanket, cover
die	Bettwäsche	bed linen
die	Birne, -n	(light) bulb
die	Bratpfanne, -n	frying pan
die	Elektrizität	electricity
die	Kerze, -n	candle

IMPORTANT WORDS (neuter)

das	Federbett, -en	continental quilt
das	Feuer	fire
das	Gas	gas
das	Geschirr	crockery; pots and pans
das	Kissen	cushion; pillow
das	Kopfkissen	pillow
das	Putzen	cleaning
das	Rezept, -e	recipe
das	Shampoo, -s	shampoo
das	Spülbecken	sink
das	Tablett, -e	tray
das	Waschbecken	washbasin

USEFUL WORDS *(masculine)*

der	**Besen**	broom
der	**Bettvorleger**	bedside rug
der	**Dampfkochtopf, ⸚e**	pressure cooker
der	**Deckel**	lid
der	**Eimer**	bucket
der	**Griff, -e**	handle (*of door etc*)
der	**Handbesen** *or* der **Handfeger**	brush
der	**Heizkörper**	radiator
der	**Henkel**	handle (*of jug etc*)
der	**Kachelofen, ⸚**	tiled stove
der	**Kessel**	kettle
der	**Kleiderbügel**	coat hanger
der	**Krug, ⸚e**	jug
der	**Mixer**	(electric) blender
der	**Müll**	rubbish, refuse
der	**Mülleimer**	dustbin
der	**Papierkorb, ⸚e**	waste paper basket
der	**Pinsel**	paintbrush; brush
der	**Rasierpinsel**	shaving brush
der	**Schmutz**	dirt
der	**Schneebesen**	whisk, egg beater
der	**Schwamm, ⸚e**	sponge
der	**Staub**	dust
der	**Staubsauger**	vacuum cleaner, Hoover®
der	**Teppichboden, ⸚**	fitted carpet
der	**Toaster**	toaster
der	**Ziergegenstand, ⸚e**	ornament

USEFUL PHRASES

sein eigenes Zimmer haben to have a room of one's own
die Tür aufmachen/zumachen, die Tür öffnen/schließen to open/
   close the door
das Zimmer betreten to go into the room
putzen to clean; abstauben to dust; staubsaugen to hoover
bürsten to brush; waschen to wash; bügeln to iron

USEFUL WORDS (feminine)

die	Brücke, -n	(narrow) rug
die	Daunendecke, -n	eiderdown
die	Fußmatte, -n	doormat
die	Heizdecke, -n	electric blanket
die	Kaffeemühle, -n	coffee grinder
die	Leiter, -n	ladder
die	Matte, -n	mat
die	Nackenrolle, -n	bolster
die	Rasierklinge, -n	razor blade
die	Röhre, -n	pipe
die	Rührmaschine, -n	(electric) mixer
die	Satellitenantenne, -n	satellite dish
die	Steppdecke, -n	(continental) quilt
die	Tapete, -n	wallpaper
die	Vase, -n	vase
die	Waage, -n	(set of) scales
die	Wäscheschleuder, -n	spin dryer

USEFUL WORDS (neuter)

das	Abwaschtuch, ̈er	dish cloth
das	Bügelbrett, -er	ironing board or table
das	Bügeleisen	iron
das	Dampfbügeleisen	steam iron
das	Gemälde	painting, picture
das	Geschirrtuch, ̈er	dish cloth; tea towel
das	Polster	cushion; pillow
das	Rohr, -e	pipe
das	Seifenpulver	soap powder
das	Staubtuch, ̈er	duster

ESSENTIAL WORDS *(masculine)*

der	Absender (Abs.)	sender
der	Anruf, -e	telephone call
der	Bescheid, -e	information
der	Brief, -e	letter
der	Briefkasten, ⁝	postbox, pillar box
der	Briefträger	postman
der	Cent, -s	cent
der	Euro, -s	euro
der	Fernsprecher	telephone
der	Geldbeutel	purse
der	Kugelschreiber; der Kuli, -s	ballpoint pen, Biro®
der	Kurs, -e	rate
der	Name, -n	name
der	Polizist, -en	policeman
der	Preis, -e	price, cost
der	(Reise)scheck, -s	(traveller's) cheque
der	Schalter	counter
der	(Telefon)hörer	(telephone) receiver
der	Umschlag, ⁝e	envelope
der	Vorname, -n	first name, Christian name

USEFUL PHRASES

entschuldigen Sie bitte – wo ist der nächste Briefkasten? excuse me – where is the nearest postbox?

kennst du dich hier aus? do you know this place (well)?

wo bekomme ich Auskunft? where can I get some information?

ist es (nach Bremen) noch weit? do we have far to go (to Bremen)?

wie komme ich zum Bahnhof? how do I get to the station?

geradeaus straight on

die erste Straße links the first street on the left

die dritte Straße rechts the third street on the right

links/rechts abbiegen to turn left/right

2 Kilometer nördlich der Stadtmitte 2 kilometres north of the town centre

ESSENTIAL WORDS *(feminine)*

die	**Adresse, -n** *or* **die Anschrift, -en**	address
die	**Ansichtskarte, -n**	picture postcard
die	**Auskunft, ¨e**	information; directory enquiries
die	**Bank, -en**	bank
die	**Bezahlung, -en**	payment
die	**Briefkarte, -n**	letter card
die	**Briefmarke, -n**	(postage) stamp
die	**Einladung, -en**	invitation
die	**E-Mail, -s**	e-mail
die	**(Hand)tasche, -n**	(hand)bag
die	**Kasse, -n**	cash desk; check-out; till
die	**Münze, -n**	coin
die	**Polizei**	police
die	**Polizeiwache, -n**	police station
die	**Polizistin**	policewoman
die	**Post**	post, mail
die	**Postkarte, -n**	postcard
die	**Reparatur, -en**	repair, repairing
die	**Rückgabe, -n**	return
die	**SIM-Karte, -n**	SIM card
die	**SMS**	text message
die	**Sparkasse, -n**	savings bank
die	**Taste, -n**	(push-)button
die	**Telefonzelle, -n**	callbox, telephone box
die	**Unterschrift, -en**	signature
die	**Vorwahlnummer, -n**	dialling code
die	**Wechselstube, -n**	bureau de change

USEFUL PHRASES

ich habe meine Tasche verloren – hat jemand sie gefunden? I've lost my
 bag – has anyone found it?
beschreiben to describe
liegen lassen to leave behind; klauen to pinch
ein Formular ausfüllen to fill in a form
der Bank *(dat)* Bescheid sagen to inform the bank

ESSENTIAL WORDS *(neuter)*

das	**Briefpapier, -e**	writing paper
das	**Fax(gerät), -e**	fax
das	**Formular, -e**	form
das	**Fundbüro, -s**	lost property office
das	**Handy, -s**	mobile phone
das	**Kleingeld**	small change
das	**Mobiltelefon, -e**	mobile phone
das	**Päckchen**	package, *(small)* parcel
das	**Paket, -e**	parcel, package
das	**Portemonnaie, -s**	purse
das	**Postamt, ̈er**	post office
das	**Postwertzeichen**	postage stamp
das	**Problem, -e**	problem
das	**Scheckheft, -e**	cheque book
das	**Telefon, -e**	telephone
das	**Telefonbuch, ̈er**	telephone directory
das	**Verkehrsamt, ̈er**	tourist information office

USEFUL PHRASES

einen Brief schreiben to write a letter

aufgeben to send, post; senden, schicken to send

zur Post gehen to go to the post office

den Brief einwerfen to post the letter (in postbox)

ein Paket aufgeben to hand in a parcel

faxen to fax

einige Briefmarken kaufen to buy some stamps

was ist das Porto für einen Brief nach Schottland? how much is a letter
  to Scotland?

3 Briefmarken zu 80 Cent 3 80-cent stamps

ist Post für mich da? is there any mail for me?

erwarten to expect

bekommen, erhalten to get, receive

zurückschicken to send back

mit Luftpost by airmail

portofrei freepost; postlagernd poste restante

IMPORTANT WORDS (masculine)

der **Anschluss, ⁻e**	(telephone) extension
der **Fehler**	fault; mistake, error
der **ISDN-Anschluss, ⁻e**	ISDN connection
der **Luftpostbrief, -e**	airmail letter
der **Personalausweis, -e**	identity card
der **Postbeamte, -n**	counter clerk
der **Zeuge, -n**	witness

IMPORTANT WORDS (feminine)

die **(Bank)note, -n**	(bank)note
die **Beschreibung, -en**	description
die **Brieftasche, -n**	wallet
die **Faxnummer, -n**	fax number
die **Geldstrafe, -n**	fine
die **Heimat, -en**	home (town/country etc)
die **Leerung, -en**	collection (of mail)
die **Luftpost**	airmail
die **Nummer, -n**	number
die **Postbeamtin**	counter clerk
die **Postgebühr, -en**	postage
die **Prepaidkarte, -n**	prepaid card
die **Scheckkarte, -n**	cheque card
die **Telefonnummer, -n**	phone number
die **Verabredung, -en**	date, appointment
die **Verbindung, -en**	line, connection
die **Währung, -en**	currency

USEFUL PHRASES

ich möchte einen Scheck einlösen I'd like to cash a cheque
unterschreiben to sign
ich möchte Pfunde (in Euro) umtauschen I'd like to change some pounds
(into euros)
können Sie mir einen Euro wechseln? can you give me change of a euro?
wie viel Geld willst du wechseln? how much money do you want to change?
ich habe kein Kleingeld I don't have any (small) change
bar bezahlen to pay in cash
ein Scheck über 100 Pfund a cheque for £100

IMPORTANT WORDS (neuter)

das	**Bargeld**	cash
das	**Ferngespräch, -e**	trunk call
das	**Geschlecht, -er**	sex
das	**Missverständnis, -se**	misunderstanding
das	**Ortsgespräch, -e**	local call
das	**Pfund Sterling**	pound sterling
das	**R-Gespräch, -e**	reverse-charge call
das	**Telefongespräch, -e**	phone call
das	**Telegramm, -e**	telegram, cable
das	**Termin, -e**	(doctor's etc) appointment

USEFUL PHRASES

jdn anrufen, mit jdm telefonieren **to phone** or **call sb**
den Hörer abheben **to lift the receiver**
ein R-Gespräch führen **to make a reverse-charge call**
die Nummer suchen/wählen **to look up/dial the number**
können Sie mir die Vorwahlnummer sagen? **can you tell me the dialling code?**
drücken **to press**
das Telefon läutet **the phone rings**
wer ist am Apparat? **who's speaking?**
hallo, hier ist ... **hello, this is ...**
kann ich Peter sprechen? **could I speak to Peter?**
bleiben Sie am Apparat **hold on, please**
eine Nachricht hinterlassen **to leave a message**
besetzt **engaged;** außer Betrieb **out of order**
Sie sind falsch verbunden **you have the wrong number**
ich habe mich verwählt **I dialled the wrong number**
danke für den Anruf **thank you for calling**
ich rufe Sie zurück **I'll call you back**
die Verbindung ist sehr schlecht **it's a bad line**
den Hörer auflegen or einhängen **to replace the receiver**
mailen **to e-mail;** simsen **to text**
eine SMS-Nachricht schicken **to send a text message**

USEFUL WORDS (masculine)

der	Einschreibebrief, -e	registered letter
der	Empfänger	addressee
der	Stempel	postmark

USEFUL WORDS (feminine)

die	Blockschrift	block capitals (pl)
die	Drucksache, -n	printed matter
die	Kaution, -en	deposit
die	Postanweisung, -en	postal order
die	Postleitzahl, -en	postcode
die	Steuer, -n	tax

USEFUL WORDS (neuter)

das	Branchenverzeichnis, -se	Yellow Pages® (pl)
das	Einschreiben	registered letter
das	Einwickelpapier	wrapping paper
das	Konto, Konten	account
das	Packpapier	brown paper, wrapping paper
das	Porto	postage

USEFUL PHRASES

sprechen Sie Englisch? **do you speak English?**
was heißt das auf Deutsch? **what's that in German?**
könnten Sie das bitte wiederholen? **could you repeat that please?**
verstehen, kapieren **to understand**
wie schreibt man das? **how do you spell that?**
soll ich das buchstabieren? **shall I spell that for you?**
Lieber Franz **Dear Franz;** Liebe Bettina **Dear Bettina**
Sehr geehrter Herr Müller **Dear Mr Müller;** Sehr geehrte Frau Brown
    Dear Mrs Brown
Sehr geehrte Damen und Herren **Dear Sir or Madam**
Mit freundlichen Grüßen **Yours sincerely**
Viele Grüße **Love, Best wishes**
Hochachtungsvoll **Yours faithfully**

ESSENTIAL WORDS (*masculine*)

der	**Ausweis, -e**	identity card
der	**Polizist, -en**	policeman
der	**Reisescheck, -s**	traveller's cheque
der	**Scheck, -s**	cheque
der	**Terrorismus**	terrorism

ESSENTIAL WORDS (*feminine*)

die	**Auskunft, ¨e**	information; particulars (*pl*)
die	**Ausweiskarte, -n**	identity card
die	**Bank, -en**	bank
die	**Polizei**	police
die	**Polizistin**	policewoman
die	**Tasche, -n**	bag

ESSENTIAL WORDS (*neuter*)

das	**Fundbüro, -s**	lost property office
das	**Geld, -er**	money
das	**Portemonnaie, -s**	purse

USEFUL PHRASES

verunglücken to have an accident
jdn überfahren to run sb over
verletzt injured; verwundet wounded
betrunken drunk
Notruf (110) emergency phone number
versichert sein to be insured
Hilfe! help!; haltet den Dieb! stop thief!
Feuer! fire!; Hände hoch! hands up!
Angst haben to be afraid
stehlen to steal; klauen to pinch; rauben to rob
eine Bank überfallen to rob a bank
entführen to kidnap; to hijack
verschwinden to disappear
die Polizei rufen to send for the police
retten to rescue; entkommen to escape; strafen to punish

IMPORTANT WORDS *(masculine)*

der	Bandit, -en	bandit
der	Demonstrant, -en	demonstrator
der	Detektiv, -e	detective
der	Dieb, -e	thief
der	Diebstahl, -̈e	theft
der	Entführer	kidnapper; hijacker
der	Gangster, -s	gangster
die	Geschworenen *(pl)*	jury
der	Privatdetektiv, -e	private detective
der	Retter	rescuer
der	Revolver	gun, revolver
der	Rowdy, -s	hooligan
der	Sicherheitsbeamte, -n	security guard
der	Streit, -e	argument, dispute
der	Taschendieb, -e	pickpocket
der	Terrorist, -en	terrorist
	Tote(r), -n	dead man/woman
der	Überfall, -̈e	raid; attack
der	Unfall, -̈e	accident
der	Zeuge, -n	witness

IMPORTANT WORDS *(neuter)*

das	Bargeld	cash, ready money
das	Gefängnis, -se	prison
das	Gericht, -e	court
das	Gesetz, -e	law
das	Recht, -e	right

USEFUL PHRASES

demonstrieren to demonstrate
ein Gebäude (in die Luft) sprengen to blow up a building
erschießen to shoot (dead)
töten to kill; ermorden to murder
verhaften to arrest; ins Gefängnis kommen to go to jail
schuldig guilty; unschuldig innocent

IMPORTANT WORDS *(feminine)*

die	**Armee, -n**	army
die	**Atomwaffe, -n**	atomic weapon
die	**Bande, -n**	band, gang
die	**Beschreibung, -en**	description
die	**Bombe, -n**	bomb
die	**Brieftasche, -n**	wallet
die	**Demonstrantin**	demonstrator
die	**Demonstration, -en**	demonstration
die	**Diebin**	thief
die	**Droge, -n**	drug
die	**Erlaubnis, -se**	permission; permit
die	**Gefahr, -en**	danger, risk
die	**Geldstrafe, -n**	fine
die	**Notdienste** *(pl)*	emergency services
die	**Pflicht, -en**	duty
die	**Pistole, -n**	gun, pistol
die	**Rettung, -en**	rescue
die	**Terroristin**	terrorist
die	**Todesstrafe, -n**	death penalty
die	**Untersuchung, -en**	inquiry, investigation
die	**Zeugin**	witness

USEFUL WORDS *(neuter)*

das	**Gewehr, -e**	gun, rifle
das	**Heer, -e**	army
das	**Rauschgift, -e**	drug
das	**(Todes)urteil, -e**	(death) sentence
das	**Verbrechen**	crime
das	**Zuchthaus, -häuser**	(top-security) prison

USEFUL WORDS *(masculine)*

der	Beweis, -e	evidence, proof
der	Brand, ⸚e	fire
der	Einbrecher	burglar
der	Einbruch, ⸚e	burglary, break-in
der	Feind, -e	enemy
	Gefangene(r), -n	prisoner
der	Gefängniswärter	prison guard
der	Gerichtshof, ⸚e	law court
der	Identitätsdiebstahl, ⸚e	identity theft
der	Mord, -e	murder
der	Mörder	murderer, killer
der	Prozess, -e	trial, lawsuit
der	Raub	robbery
der	Räuber	robber
der	Raubüberfall, ⸚e	robbery with violence
der	(Rechts)anwalt, ⸚e	lawyer, barrister
der	Spion, -e	spy
der	Verbrecher	criminal
	Verdächtige(r), -n	suspect

USEFUL WORDS *(feminine)*

die	Alarmanlage, -n	burglar alarm
die	Belohnung, -en	reward
die	Fahrerflucht	hit-and-run driving
die	Festnahme, -n	arrest
die	Flucht, -en	escape
die	Haft	custody
die	Handschellen *(pl)*	handcuffs
die	Justiz	justice
die	Leiche, -n	corpse, body
die	(Polizei)wache, -n	police station
die	Regierung, -en	government
die	Schuld	guilt; fault
die	Unschuld	innocence
die	Verhaftung, -en	arrest
die	Versicherungspolice, -n	insurance policy

ESSENTIAL WORDS (*masculine*)

der **Kaugummi**	chewing gum
der **Stein, -e**	stone, rock

ESSENTIAL WORDS (*neuter*)

das **Aluminium**	aluminium
das **Benzin**	petrol
das **Dieselöl**	diesel oil
das **Gas**	gas
das **Glas**	glass
das **Gummiband, ̈er**	rubber band; elastic
das **Leder**	leather
das **Öl, -e**	oil
das **Papier, -e**	paper

USEFUL PHRASES

eine Baumwollbluse a cotton blouse
ein Seidenschal (*m*) a silk scarf
ein Holzstuhl (*m*) a wooden chair
ein Strohhut (*m*) a straw hat
ein Pelzmantel (*m*) a fur coat
ein Wollpullover (*m*) a woollen jumper
ein Pappkarton (*m*) a cardboard box
ein Lammfellmantel (*m*) a sheepskin coat
eine Tasche aus Leder a leather bag
die Tasche ist aus Leder the bag is made of leather
eine Vase aus Ton an earthenware vase
die Vase ist aus Ton the vase is made of earthenware
eisern, Eisen- iron
golden, Gold- gold, golden
hölzern, Holz- wooden
marmorn, Marmor- marble
silbern, Silber- silver
echt real, genuine
kostbar precious; teuer costly, expensive

IMPORTANT WORDS *(masculine)*

der	**Aufkleber**	sticker, label
der	**Denim**	denim
der	**Fleck, -e**	mark, spot
der	**Gips**	plaster; plaster of Paris
der	**Jeansstoff, -e**	denim
der	**Klebstoff, -e**	glue
der	**Kord**	cord, corduroy
der	**Kunststoff, -e**	synthetic
der	**Polyester**	polyester
der	**Stahl**	steel
der	**Stoff, -e**	cloth, material

IMPORTANT WORDS *(feminine)*

die	**Baumwolle**	cotton
die	**Bronze**	bronze
die	**Gebrauchsanweisung, -en**	directions for use *(pl)*
die	**Seide**	silk

IMPORTANT WORDS *(neuter)*

das	**Blei**	lead
das	**Gold**	gold
das	*or* der **Gummi**	rubber; gum
das	**Holz, ¨er**	wood
das	**Material, -ien**	material(s)
das	**Metall, -e**	metal
das	**Nylon**	nylon
das	**Petroleum**	paraffin
das	**Plastik**	plastic
das	**Seidenpapier**	tissue paper
das	**Silber**	silver
das	**Silberpapier**	silver paper
das	**Stroh**	straw
das	**Vinyl**	vinyl
das	**Wildleder**	suede

USEFUL WORDS *(masculine)*

der	Backstein, -e	brick
der	Beton	concrete
der	Bindfaden, ∹	string
der	Draht, ∹e	wire
der	Faden, ∹	thread
der	Kalk	lime
der	Karton, -s	cardboard; cardboard box
der	Kautschuk	rubber *(substance)*
der	Kleb(e)streifen	adhesive tape
der	Marmor	marble
der	Pelz, -e	fur
der	Samt	velvet
der	Satin	satin
der	Schaumgummi	foam rubber
der	Tesafilm®	Sellotape®
der	Ton	clay
der	Tweed	tweed
der	Zement	cement
der	Ziegelstein, -e *or* der Ziegel	brick
der	Zustand, ∹e	condition

USEFUL PHRASES

in gutem/schlechtem Zustand **in good/bad condition**
„trocken aufbewahren *or* lagern" **"keep dry"**
etw chemisch reinigen **to dry-clean sth**

USEFUL WORDS *(feminine)*

die **Flüssigkeit, -en**	liquid
die **Kohle**	coal
die **Leinwand**	canvas
die **Pappe, -n**	cardboard
die **Plastikfolie, -n**	clingfilm
die **Schnur, ̈-e**	cord, string
die **Spitze, -n**	lace
die **Strickwaren** *(pl)*	knitwear
die **Watte**	cotton wool
die **Wolle**	wool

USEFUL WORDS *(neuter)*

das **Acryl**	acrylic
das **Blech**	tin
das **Eisen**	iron
das **Fell, -e**	fur, coat
das **Kristall**	crystal
das **Kupfer**	copper
das **Leinen**	linen
das **Messing**	brass
das **Porzellan**	porcelain, china
das **Schaffell**	sheepskin
das **Segeltuch**	sailcloth, canvas
das **Seil, -e**	rope; cable
das **Stanniolpapier**	tinfoil
das **Steingut**	earthenware
das **Styropor**	polystyrene
das **Wachs**	wax
das **Zinn**	pewter; tin

ESSENTIAL + IMPORTANT WORDS *(masculine)*

der	**Jazz**	jazz
der	**Musiker**	musician
der	**Triangel**	triangle
der	**Zuhörer**	listener; *(pl)* audience

ESSENTIAL + IMPORTANT WORDS *(feminine)*

die	**Blaskapelle, -n**	brass band
die	**Blockflöte, -n**	recorder
die	**Flöte, -n**	flute
die	**Geige, -n**	violin, fiddle
die	**Gitarre, -n**	guitar
die	**Gruppe, -n**	group
die	**Kapelle, -n**	band, orchestra
die	**Klarinette, -n**	clarinet
die	**Musik**	music
die	**Note, -n**	note; *(pl)* music
die	**Oboe, -n**	oboe
die	**Taste, -n**	(piano) key
die	**Trompete, -n**	trumpet

IMPORTANT WORDS *(neuter)*

das	**Akkordeon, -s**	accordion
das	**Bügelhorn, ⁻er**	bugle
das	**Cello, -s** *or* **Celli**	cello
das	**Horn, ⁻er**	horn
das	**Klavier, -e**	piano
das	**Konzert, -e**	concert; concerto
das	**(Musik)instrument, -e**	(musical) instrument
das	**Orchester**	orchestra; band
das	**Saxophon, -e**	saxophone
das	**Schlagzeug, -e**	drums *(pl)*
das	**Xylophon, -e**	xylophone

USEFUL PHRASES

Klavier/Gitarre spielen to play the piano/the guitar
die Schlagermusik pop music; die klassische Musik classical music;
die Blasmusik brass band music

USEFUL WORDS (masculine)

der	Akkord, -e	chord
der	Chor, ⁻e	choir; chorus
der	Dirigent, -en	conductor
der	Dudelsack, ⁻e	bagpipes (pl)
der	Flügel	grand piano
der	Kontrabass, -bässe	double bass
der	Solist, -en	soloist
der	Taktstock, -stöcke	(conductor's) baton
der	Ton, ⁻e	note

USEFUL WORDS (feminine)

die	Harfe, -n	harp
die	Konzerthalle, -n	concert hall
die	Mundharmonika, -s or -ken	mouth organ, harmonica
die	Musikkapelle, -n	band (circus, military etc)
die	Oper, -n	opera; opera house
die	Orgel, -n	organ
die	Posaune, -n	trombone
die	Querflöte, -n	flute
die	Saite, -n	string
die	Solistin	soloist
die	Tastatur, -en	keyboard
die	Tonart, -en	(musical) key
die	(große) Trommel, (-n) -n	(big, bass) drum
die	Violine, -n	violin
die	Ziehharmonika, -s	concertina; accordion

USEFUL WORDS (neuter)

das	Becken	cymbals (pl)
das	Fagott, -s or -e	bassoon
das	Jagdhorn, ⁻er	bugle; hunting horn
das	Opernhaus, -häuser	opera house
das	Streichorchester	string orchestra
das	Tamburin, -e	tambourine
das	Violoncello, -s or -celli	violoncello
das	Waldhorn, ⁻er	French horn

CARDINAL NUMBERS

nought	0	null
one	1	eins
two	2	zwei
three	3	drei
four	4	vier
five	5	fünf
six	6	sechs
seven	7	sieben
eight	8	acht
nine	9	neun
ten	10	zehn
eleven	11	elf
twelve	12	zwölf
thirteen	13	dreizehn
fourteen	14	vierzehn
fifteen	15	fünfzehn
sixteen	16	sechzehn
seventeen	17	siebzehn
eighteen	18	achtzehn
nineteen	19	neunzehn
twenty	20	zwanzig
twenty-one	21	einundzwanzig
twenty-two	22	zweiundzwanzig
twenty-three	23	dreiundzwanzig
thirty	30	dreißig
thirty-one	31	einunddreißig
thirty-two	32	zweiunddreißig
forty	40	vierzig
fifty	50	fünfzig
sixty	60	sechzig
seventy	70	siebzig
eighty	80	achtzig
ninety	90	neunzig
ninety-nine	99	neunundneunzig
a (or one) hundred	100	hundert

CARDINAL NUMBERS (*continued*)

a hundred and one	101	hunderteins
a hundred and two	102	hundertzwei
a hundred and ten	110	hundertzehn
a hundred and eighty-two	182	hundertzweiundachtzig
two hundred	200	zweihundert
two hundred and one	201	zweihunderteins
two hundred and two	202	zweihundertzwei
three hundred	300	dreihundert
four hundred	400	vierhundert
five hundred	500	fünfhundert
six hundred	600	sechshundert
seven hundred	700	siebenhundert
eight hundred	800	achthundert
nine hundred	900	neunhundert
a (*or* one) thousand	1000	(ein)tausend
a thousand and one	1001	tausendundeins
a thousand and two	1002	tausendundzwei
two thousand	2000	zweitausend
ten thousand	10 000	zehntausend
a (*or* one) hundred thousand	100 000	hunderttausend
a (*or* one) million	1 000 000	eine Million
two million	2 000 000	zwei Millionen

USEFUL PHRASES

1979 neunzehnhundertneunundsiebzig
2001 zweitausendundeins

gerade/ungerade Zahlen **even/odd numbers**
50 Prozent **50 per cent**

ORDINAL NUMBERS

These can be masculine, feminine or neuter, and take the appropriate endings.

first	der Erste
second	der Zweite
third	der Dritte
fourth	der Vierte
fifth	der Fünfte
sixth	der Sechste
seventh	der Siebte
eighth	der Achte
ninth	der Neunte
tenth	der Zehnte
eleventh	der Elfte
twelfth	der Zwölfte
thirteenth	der Dreizehnte
fourteenth	der Vierzehnte
fifteenth	der Fünfzehnte
sixteenth	der Sechzehnte
seventeenth	der Siebzehnte
eighteenth	der Achtzehnte
nineteenth	der Neunzehnte
twentieth	der Zwanzigste
twenty-first	der Einundzwanzigste
twenty-second	der Zweiundzwanzigste
thirtieth	der Dreißigste
thirty-first	der Einunddreißigste
fortieth	der Vierzigste
fiftieth	der Fünfzigste
sixtieth	der Sechzigste
seventieth	der Siebzigste
eightieth	der Achtzigste
ninetieth	der Neunzigste
hundredth	der Hundertste
hundred and first	der Hunderterste
hundred and tenth	der Hundertzehnte

ORDINAL NUMBERS *(continued)*

two hundredth	der Zweihundertste
three hundredth	der Dreihundertste
four hundredth	der Vierhundertste
five hundredth	der Fünfhundertste
six hundredth	der Sechshundertste
seven hundredth	der Siebenhundertste
eight hundredth	der Achthundertste
nine hundredth	der Neunhundertste
thousandth	der Tausendste
two thousandth	der Zweitausendste
millionth	der Millionste
two millionth	der Zweimillionste

FRACTIONS

a half	halb, die Hälfte
one and a half kilos	eineinhalb Kilos, anderthalb Kilos
two and a half kilos	zweieinhalb Kilos
a third	ein Drittel *(nt)*
two thirds	zwei Drittel
a quarter	ein Viertel *(nt)*
three quarters	drei Viertel
a sixth	ein Sechstel *(nt)*
five and five sixths	fünf und fünf Sechstel
an eighth	ein Achtel *(nt)*
a twelfth	ein Zwölftel *(nt)*
a twentieth	ein Zwanzigstel *(nt)*
a hundredth	ein Hundertstel *(nt)*
a thousandth	ein Tausendstel *(nt)*
a millionth	ein Millionstel *(nt)*

USEFUL PHRASES

zum x-ten Mal for the umpteenth time
ein Millionär a millionaire
(0, 4) null Komma vier (0.4) nought point four
die Flasche war drei viertel leer the bottle was three-quarters empty

NUMBERS AND QUANTITIES

der	Becher (Joghurt)	pot (of yogurt)
ein	bisschen	a little (bit of)
die	Büchse, -n	tin, can
der	*or* das Deziliter	decilitre
das	Dutzend	dozen
	Dutzende von	dozens of
	etwas	a little (bit of)
das	Fass, ⁻er	barrel
die	Flasche, -n (Wein)	bottle (of wine)
das	Glas, ⁻er (Milch)	glass (of milk)
das	Glas, ⁻er Marmelade	jar *or* pot of jam
eine	Halbe	a half (*litre of beer etc*)
ein	halbes Dutzend/	half-a-dozen/-pound, a
	Pfund	half dozen/pound
ein	halbes Kilo	half a kilo
ein	halber Liter	half a litre
die	Handvoll (Münzen)	handful (of coins)
der	Haufen	heap, pile
ein	Haufen	heaps of
	Hunderte von	hundreds of
	hundert Gramm Käse	a hundred grammes of cheese
die	Kanne, -n (Kaffee)	pot (of coffee)
das	Kilo(gramm)	kilo(gramme)
ein	Kleines	a half pint (*of beer etc*)
das	Knäuel Wolle *or* das Wollknäuel	ball of wool
der	*or* das Liter	litre
die	Menge, -n	crowd; heaps of
der	*or* das Meter (Stoff)	metre (of cloth)
das	Paar (Schuhe)	pair (of shoes)
das	Päckchen	packet
die	Packung Keks/	packet of biscuits/
	Zigaretten	cigarettes
das	Pfund (Kartoffeln)	pound (of potatoes)
die	Portion, -en (Eis)	portion *or* helping (of ice cream)

NUMBERS AND QUANTITIES *(continued)*

der	Riegel Seife	cake *or* bar of soap
der	Riegel Schokolade	bar of chocolate, chocolate bar
die	Schachtel, -n	box; packet (*of cigarettes*)
die	Schar, -en	group, band
die	Scheibe, -n (Brot)	slice (of bread)
die	Schüssel, -n	bowl, dish
der	Stapel	pile
das	Stück Zucker	lump of sugar
das	Stück Kuchen	piece *or* slice of cake
das	Stück Papier	bit *or* piece of paper
die	Tafel (-n) Schokolade	bar of chocolate
die	Tasse (voll)	cup(ful)
	Tausende von	thousands of
der	Teller	plate
das	Viertel(pfund)	quarter(-pound)
ein	wenig	a little (bit) of
der	Würfel Zucker	lump of sugar
der	Würfel Margarine	half a pound of margarine (*in cube shape*)

USEFUL PHRASES

für das Dutzend/das Hundert/das Tausend **per dozen/hundred/thousand,** (for) a dozen/a hundred/a thousand

ESSENTIAL WORDS *(masculine)*

der **Artikel**	article
der **Ohrring, -e**	earring
der **Rasierapparat, -e**	razor
der **Ring, -e**	ring
der **Schlüsselring, -e**	key-ring
der **Schmuck**	jewellery

ESSENTIAL WORDS *(feminine)*

die **Armbanduhr, -en**	(wrist) watch
die **Haarbürste, -n**	hairbrush
die **Halskette, -n**	necklace
die **Kette, -n**	chain
die **Rasiercreme, -s**	shaving cream
die **Sache, -n**	thing
die **Schönheit**	beauty
die **Seife, -n**	soap
die **Zahnbürste, -n**	toothbrush
die **Zahnpasta, -pasten**	toothpaste

ESSENTIAL + IMPORTANT WORDS *(neuter)*

das **Armband, ̈-er**	bracelet
das **Deo, -s**	deodorant
das **Gold**	gold
das **Haarwaschmittel**	shampoo
das **Handtuch, ̈-er**	towel
das **Juwel, -en**	jewel; *(pl)* jewels, jewellery
das **Make-up**	foundation; make-up
das **Parfüm, -s** *or* **-e**	perfume, scent
das **Rasierwasser**	after-shave
das **Shampoo, -s**	shampoo
das **Silber**	silver
das **Taschengeld**	pocket money
das **Toilettenwasser**	toilet water

USEFUL PHRASES
baden to have a bath; duschen to have a shower
sich die Zähne putzen to brush one's teeth

IMPORTANT WORDS *(masculine)*

der **Ehering, -e**	wedding ring
der **Gesichtspuder**	face powder
der **Kamm, ⁻e**	comb
der **Schönheitssalon, -s**	beauty salon
der **Spiegel**	mirror
der **Tampon, -s**	tampon

IMPORTANT WORDS *(feminine)*

die **(Damen)binde**	sanitary towel
die **Gesichtscreme, -s**	face cream
die **Kosmetik**	cosmetics *(pl)*, make-up
die **Perle, -n**	pearl; bead
die **Perlenkette, -n**	beads, string of beads

USEFUL WORDS *(masculine)*

der **Anhänger**	pendant
der **Edelstein, -e**	gem, precious stone
der **Lidschatten**	eyeshadow
der **Lippenstift, -e**	lipstick
der **Lockenwickler**	curler, roller
der **Nagellack**	nail varnish, nail polish
der **Nagellackentferner**	nail varnish remover
der **Trauring, -e**	wedding ring
der **Waschbeutel**	toilet bag
der **Waschlappen**	face flannel

USEFUL WORDS *(feminine)*

die **Brosche, -n**	brooch
die **Frisur, -en**	hairstyle
die **Krawattennadel, -n**	tie-pin
die **Perücke, -n**	wig
die **Puderdose, -n**	(powder) compact
die **Schminke, -n**	make-up
die **Wimperntusche**	mascara

USEFUL PHRASES
sich rasieren to shave; kämmen to comb; bürsten to brush

ESSENTIAL WORDS (*masculine*)

der **Baum, Bäume**	tree
der **Blumentopf, ⸚e**	flower pot
der **Garten, ⸚**	garden
der **Gärtner**	gardener
der **Gemüsegarten, ⸚**	vegetable garden
der **Grund**	ground
der **Obstgarten, ⸚**	orchard
der **Regen**	rain
der **Sonnenschein**	sunshine
der **Stein, -e**	stone, rock

ESSENTIAL WORDS (*feminine*)

die **Biene, -n**	bee
die **Blume, -n**	flower
die **Erde, -n**	earth, soil
die **(Garten)bank, ⸚e**	(garden) seat *or* bench
die **Gartentür, -en**	garden gate
die **Rose, -n**	rose
die **Sonne**	sun
die **Wespe, -n**	wasp

ESSENTIAL WORDS (*neuter*)

das **Blatt, ⸚er**	leaf
das **Gärtnern**	gardening
das **Gemüse**	vegetable(s)
das **Gras**	grass

USEFUL PHRASES

Blumen pflanzen to plant flowers
die Pflanzen wachsen the plants grow
gießen to water
pflücken to pick
ein Strauß Rosen/Veilchen, ein Rosenstrauß/Veilchenstrauß
  a bunch of roses/violets

IMPORTANT WORDS (masculine)

der	Boden, ⸚	ground, soil
der	Busch, ⸚e	bush, shrub
der	Krokus, - or -se	crocus
der	Pfad, -e	path
der	Rasen	lawn; turf
der	Schatten	shadow; shade
der	Stamm, ⸚e	trunk
der	Steingarten, ⸚	rockery, rock garden
der	Weg, -e	path
der	Wurm, ⸚er	worm

IMPORTANT WORDS (feminine)

die	Chrysantheme, -n	chrysanthemum
die	Dahlie, -n	dahlia
die	Hütte, -n	hut, shed
die	Hyazinthe, -n	hyacinth
die	Lilie, -n	lily
die	Orchidee, -n	orchid
die	Pflanze, -n	plant
die	Sonnenblume, -n	sunflower
die	Tulpe, -n	tulip

IMPORTANT WORDS (neuter)

das	Gartenhaus, -häuser	summerhouse
das	Laub(werk)	leaves (pl), foliage
das	Unkraut	weed(s)
das	Werkzeug, -e	tool

USEFUL PHRASES

den Garten umgraben to dig the garden
den Rasen mähen to mow the lawn
im Schatten eines Baumes in the shade of a tree
im Schatten bleiben to stay in the shade
allerlei Pflanzen all kinds of plants
hier duftet es (gut) what a nice smell there is here

USEFUL WORDS *(masculine)*

der	**Ast, ⸚e**	branch
der	**Baumstamm, ⸚e**	tree trunk
der	**Blumenstrauß, (-sträuße)**	bunch or bouquet of flowers
der	**Dorn, -en**	thorn
der	**Duft, ⸚e**	perfume, scent
der	**Efeu**	ivy
der	**Flieder**	lilac
der	**Goldlack**	wallflower
der	**Halm, -e**	stalk, blade
der	**Löwenzahn**	dandelion
der	**Mohn, -e**	poppy
der	**Rasenmäher**	lawnmower
der	**Rosenstock, ⸚e**	rose bush
der	**Samen**	seed(s)
der	**Schlauch, Schläuche**	garden hose
der	**Schmetterling, -e**	butterfly
der	**Schubkarren**	wheelbarrow
der	**Stachel, -n**	thorn
der	**Stängel; der Stiel, -e**	stalk, stem
der	**Strauch, Sträucher**	shrub
der	**Strauß, Sträuße**	bunch or bouquet (of flowers)
der	**Tau**	dew
der	**Weiher**	pond
der	**Wintergarten, ⸚**	conservatory
der	**Zaun, Zäune**	fence
der	**Zweig, -e**	branch

USEFUL PHRASES

Unkraut jäten to do the weeding
die Hecke schneiden to cut the hedge
die Blätter zusammenharken to rake up the leaves
umzäunt fenced in
sonnig sunny; schattig shady

USEFUL WORDS *(feminine)*

die	**Beere, -n**	berry
die	**Blüte, -n**	blossom
die	**Butterblume, -n**	buttercup
die	**Gartenwicke, -n**	sweet pea
die	**Gießkanne, -n**	watering can
die	**Hacke, -n**	hoe
die	**Harke, -n**	rake
die	**Hecke, -n**	hedge
die	**Heckenschere, -n**	hedge-cutters, garden shears
die	**Hortensie, -n**	hydrangea
die	**Knospe, -n**	bud
die	**Leiter, -n**	ladder
die	**Margerite, -n**	daisy
die	**Narzisse, -n**	narcissus, daffodil
die	**Nelke, -n**	carnation
die	**Osterglocke, -n**	daffodil
die	**Pforte, -n**	(garden) gate
die	**Primel, -n**	primrose
die	**Rabatte, -n**	border, flower bed
die	**Walze, -n**	roller
die	**Wurzel, -n**	root

USEFUL WORDS *(neuter)*

das	**Blumenbeet, -e**	flowerbed
das	**Gänseblümchen**	daisy
das	**Geißblatt**	honeysuckle
das	**Gewächshaus, -häuser**	greenhouse
das	**Maiglöckchen**	lily of the valley
das	**Schneeglöckchen**	snowdrop
das	**Stiefmütterchen**	pansy
das	**Veilchen**	violet
das	**Vergissmeinnicht, -e**	forget-me-not

ESSENTIAL WORDS (*masculine*)

der	Ausflug, ¨e	trip, outing
der	Badeanzug, ¨e	swimming or bathing costume
der	Bikini, -s	bikini
der	Dampfer	steamer
der	Fahrgast, ¨e	passenger
der	Fisch, -e	fish
der	Fischer	fisherman
der	Hafen, ¨	port, harbour
der	Passagier, -e	passenger
der	Schwimmer	swimmer
der	Seehafen, ¨	seaport
der	Seemann, (-leute)	sailor, seaman
der	Sonnenschein	sunshine
der	Spaziergang, ¨e	walk
der	Stein, -e	stone
der	Strand, ¨e	shore, beach
der	Urlauber	holiday-maker

ESSENTIAL WORDS (*feminine*)

die	Ansichtskarte, -n	postcard
die	Badehose, -n	swimming or bathing trunks
die	Fähre, -n	ferry
die	Hafenstadt, ¨e	port
die	Insel, -n	island
die	Mannschaft, -en	crew
die	Schwimmerin	swimmer
die	See, -n	sea
die	Seekrankheit	seasickness
die	Seeluft	sea air
die	Sonne	sun
die	Sonnenbrille, -n	(pair of) sunglasses
die	Sonnencreme, -s	sun(tan) cream
die	Überfahrt, -en	crossing
die	Urlauberin	holiday-maker

ESSENTIAL WORDS *(neuter)*

das Ausland	abroad
das Bad, ⸚er	bathe *(in sea)*, swim
das Badetuch, ⸚er	(bath) towel
das Boot, -e	boat
das Fischerboot, -e	fishing boat
das Meer, -e	ocean, sea
das Picknick, -e *or* -s	picnic
das Ruder	oar; rudder
das Schiff, -e	ship, vessel
das Schwimmen	swimming
das Sonnenöl, -e	suntan oil
das Wasser	water

IMPORTANT WORDS *(masculine)*

der Anker	anchor
Badende(r), -n	bather, swimmer
der Bord, -e	board
der Horizont	horizon
der (Meeres)boden	bottom (of the sea)
der Ozean, -e	ocean
der Prospekt, -e	leaflet, brochure
der Rettungsring, -e	lifebelt
der Sand, -e	send
der Segler	sailor, yachtsman
der Sonnenbrand, ⸚e	sunburn

USEFUL PHRASES

zwei Wochen Urlaub **two weeks' holiday**
am Meer **at the seaside**
ans Meer *or* an die See fahren **to go to the seaside**
es ist Flut/Ebbe **the tide is in/out**
schwimmen gehen **to go for a swim;** sich ausruhen **to have a rest**
sich sonnen **to sunbathe;** am Strand **on the beach**
eine Sonnenbrille tragen **to wear sunglasses**
braun werden **to get a tan**
einen Sonnenbrand bekommen **to get sunburnt**

IMPORTANT WORDS (feminine)

die	**Flagge, -n**	flag
die	**Küste, -n**	coast, shore; seaside
die	**Luftmatratze, -n**	lilo®, airbed
die	**Seglerin**	sailor, yachtswoman
die	**Vergnügungsfahrt, -en**	pleasure cruise

IMPORTANT WORDS (neuter)

das	**Reisebüro, -s**	travel agent's
das	**Segel**	sail
das	**Segeln**	sailing
das	**Teleskop, -e**	telescope
das	**Ufer**	shore (lake); bank (river)

USEFUL WORDS (masculine)

der	**Eimer**	bucket
der	**Jachthafen, ̈**	marina
der	**Kahn, ̈e**	(small) boat
der	**Kai, -e** or **-s**	quay, quayside
der	**Kieselstein, -e**	pebble
der	**Krebs, -e**	crab
der	**Leuchtturm, ̈e**	lighthouse
der	**Liegestuhl, ̈e**	deckchair
der	**Mast, -e(n)**	mast
der	**Matrose, -n**	sailor
der	**Pier, -e** or **-s**	pier
der	**Rettungsschwimmer**	lifeguard
der	**Schaum**	foam
der	**Schiffbruch, ̈e**	shipwreck
der	**Schornstein, ̈e**	funnel
der	**(See)tang, -e**	seaweed
der	**Sonnenstich, -e**	sunstroke
der	**Spaten**	spade

USEFUL WORDS *(feminine)*

die **Boje, -n**	buoy
die **Bucht, -en**	bay
die **Ebbe, -n**	low tide
die **Fahne, -n**	flag
die **Flotte, -n**	navy, fleet
die **Flut, -en**	high tide
die **Jacht, -en**	yacht
die **Klippe, -n**	cliff
die **Kreuzfahrt, -en**	cruise
die **Last, -en**	load, cargo
die **Möwe, -n**	seagull
die **Muschel(schale), -n (-n)**	shell
die **Pauschalreise, -n**	package tour
die **Sandburg, -en**	sandcastle
die **(Schiffs)ladung, -en**	cargo
die **Schwimmweste, -n**	life jacket
die **(Sonnen)bräune**	(sun)tan
die **Strömung, -en**	current
die **Welle, -n**	wave

USEFUL WORDS *(neuter)*

das **Deck, -s** *or* **-e**	deck (*of ship*)
das **Fahrgeld, -er**	fare
das **Floß, ⁻e**	raft
das **Steuer**	helm, tiller
das **Surfbrett, -er**	surfboard
das **Tretboot, -e**	pedal-boat, pedalo

USEFUL PHRASES
eine Bootsfahrt machen to go on a boat trip
an Bord gehen to go on board
ruhig calm; stürmisch stormy; bewegt choppy
seekrank werden to get seasick
untergehen to go under
ertrinken to drown

ESSENTIAL WORDS (masculine)

der	Artikel	article
der	Bäcker	baker
der	Cent, -s	cent
der	Einkauf, -käufe	shopping; purchase
der	Euro, -s	euro
der	Fahrstuhl, ⸚e	lift
der	Franken	(Swiss) franc
der	Geldbeutel	purse
der	Geschäftsmann, -leute	businessman
der	Groschen	10-pfennig piece; groschen
der	Kiosk, -e	kiosk
der	Kunde, -n	customer, client
der	Laden, ⸚	shop
der	Markt, ⸚e	market
der	Preis, -e	price
der	Rappen	centime
der	Schalter	counter (post office, bank etc)
der	Scheck, -s	cheque
der	Schein, -e	(bank)note
der	Schuhmacher	shoemaker, shoe repairer
der	Sommerschlussverkauf	summer sale
der	Supermarkt, ⸚e	supermarket

USEFUL PHRASES

einkaufen gehen to go shopping
Einkäufe machen to do the shopping
Schlange stehen to queue up
kaufen to buy; verkaufen to sell; jdn bedienen to serve sb
kann ich Ihnen behilflich sein? can I help you?
was darf es sein, bitte? what would you like?
ich möchte ... I'd like...; ich brauche ... I need ...
etw bezahlen to pay for sth
etwas stimmt nicht there's something wrong somewhere
ich möchte mich nur mal umsehen I'm just looking

ESSENTIAL WORDS (feminine)

die	Apotheke, -n	chemist's, pharmacy
die	Bäckerei, -en	bakery, baker's (shop)
die	Bank, -en	bank
die	Bibliothek, -en	library
die	Buchhandlung, -en	bookshop, bookseller's
die	Drogerie, -n	(retail) chemist's
die	Etage, -n	floor
die	Farbe, -n	colour
die	Geschäftszeit, -en	business hours
die	Größe, -n	size
die	Handlung, -en	shop
die	Kasse, -n	till; cash desk, checkout
die	Konditorei, -en	cake shop
die	Kreditkarte, -n	credit card
die	Kundin	customer, client
die	Liste, -n	list
die	Metzgerei, -en	butcher's (shop)
die	Öffnungszeit, -en	opening time
die	Post, Postämter	post office
die	Rechnung, -en	bill
die	Schachtel, -n	box
die	Schuhgröße, -n	shoe size
die	Selbstbedienung (SB)	self-service
die	Sparkasse, -n	savings bank
die	Tierhandlung, -en	pet shop
die	Tüte, -n	bag

USEFUL PHRASES
erhältlich available; ausverkauft sold out
beim Bäcker/Fleischer at the baker's/butcher's
anbieten to offer; etw probieren to try sth (taste, sample)
etw anprobieren to try sth on
das gefällt mir I like that
wählen to choose; wiegen to weigh

ESSENTIAL WORDS *(neuter)*

das	**Andenken**	souvenir
das	**Büro, -s**	office
das	**Café, -s**	café
das	**Einkaufen**	shopping
das	**Erdgeschoss, -e**	ground level, ground floor
das	**Geld**	money
das	**Geschäft, -e**	shop; trade, business; deal
das	**Geschenk, -e**	present, gift
das	**Kaufhaus, -häuser**	department store
das	**Kleingeld**	small change
das	**Portemonnaie, -s**	purse
das	**Postamt, ̈-er**	post office
das	**Restaurant, -s**	restaurant
das	**Schuhgeschäft, -e**	shoe shop
das	**Sonderangebot, -e**	bargain (offer), special offer
das	**Souvenir, -s**	souvenir
das	**Warenhaus, -häuser**	department store
das	**Wirtshaus, -häuser**	pub, inn

USEFUL PHRASES

was kostet das? what does it cost?

was macht das? what does that come to?

ich habe 15 Euro dafür bezahlt I paid 15 euros for it

einen Scheck ausstellen to write out a cheque

bar bezahlen to pay cash

Geld für Pralinen ausgeben to spend money on chocolates

zu teuer too dear; ganz billig quite cheap

kostenlos free, free of charge; umsonst for nothing

preiswert good value; ein preiswertes Angebot a bargain

das habe ich günstig bekommen I got it at a good price

das ist aber günstig! what a bargain!

Montags Ruhetag closed on Mondays

IMPORTANT WORDS (masculine)

der	Apotheker	(dispensing) chemist
der	Aufzug, ⁻e	lift
der	Ausverkauf, -käufe	sale
die	Betriebsferien (pl)	holidays (of a business)
der	Bioladen, -läden	organic food shop
der	Buchhändler	bookseller
der	Einkaufskorb, -körbe	shopping basket
der	Einkaufswagen	shopping trolley
der	Fischhändler	fishmonger
der	Fleischer	butcher
der	Friseur, -e	hairdresser
der	Händler	dealer
der	Herrenfriseur, -e	barber, men's hairdresser
der	Juwelier	jeweller
der	Kassenzettel	receipt
der	Kaufmann, -leute	merchant
der	Konditor, -en	confectioner
der	Metzger	butcher
der	Obst- und Gemüsehändler	greengrocer
der	Obsthändler	fruiterer
der	Ökoladen, -läden	wholefood shop
der	Schlussverkauf, -käufe	(end-of-season) sale
der	Sonderpreis, -e	special price
der	Tabakladen, ⁻	tobacconist's (shop)
der	Umtausch	exchange (of goods)
der	Verkauf, -käufe	sale
der	Verkäufer	salesman, shop assistant
der	Waschsalon, -s	laundrette
der	Zeitungshändler	newsagent

USEFUL PHRASES
GmbH Ltd
AG plc

IMPORTANT WORDS *(feminine)*

die	Abteilung, -en	department
die	Anprobe, -n	trying on
die	Auswahl (an + *dat*)	choice (of)
die	Brieftasche, -n	wallet
die	Firma, Firmen	firm, company
die	Fleischerei, -en	butcher's (shop)
die	Friseuse, -n	hairdresser
die	Gaststätte, -n	restaurant; pub
die	Kneipe, -n	pub
die	Kundenkarte, -n	charge card
die	Packung, -en	packet, box
die	Parfümerie, -n	perfume counter *or* shop
die	Quittung, -en	receipt
die	Schaufensterpuppe, -n	dummy, model
die	Schlange, -n	queue
die	Schreibwarenhandlung, -en	stationer's
die	Theke, -n	counter (*in café, bar etc*)
die	Verkäuferin	salesgirl, shop assistant
die	Waren (*pl*)	goods, wares

IMPORTANT WORDS *(neuter)*

das	Einkaufszentrum, -tren	shopping centre
das	Internetcafé, -s	Internet café
das	Juweliergeschäft, -e	jeweller's (shop)
das	Mediencenter	media centre
das	Milchgeschäft, -e	dairy
das	Obergeschoss, -e	upper floor
das	Produkt, -e	product; (*pl*) produce
das	Reisebüro, -s	travel agent's
das	Schaufenster	shop window
das	Untergeschoss, -e	basement

USEFUL PHRASES

einen Schaufensterbummel machen **to go window-shopping**

USEFUL WORDS (masculine)

der	Buchmacher	bookmaker, "bookie"
der	Einkaufsbummel	shopping spree
der	Eisenwarenhändler	ironmonger
der	(Flick)schuster	cobbler, shoe repairer
der	Gelegenheitskauf, -käufe	bargain
der	Grundstücksmakler	estate agent
der	Gutschein, -e	voucher
der	Handel	trade, business
der	Ladentisch, -e	counter (in shop)
der	Lebensmittelhändler	grocer
der	Optiker	optician
der	Uhrmacher	watchmaker
der	Waschsalon, -s	laundrette

USEFUL WORDS (feminine)

die	Bausparkasse, -n	building society
die	Besorgung, -en	errand; purchase
die	Bücherei, -en	library
die	Bude, -n	stall
die	Eisenwarenhandlung, -en	ironmonger's, hardware shop
die	Filiale, -n	branch
die	Garantie, -n	guarantee
die	Kragenweite, -n	collar size
die	Reinigung, -en	cleaner's
die	Rolltreppe, -n	escalator
die	Versicherungsgesellschaft, -en	insurance company
die	Videothek, -en	video shop
die	Wäscherei, -en	laundry, cleaner's

USEFUL WORDS (neuter)

das	Erzeugnis, -se	product; produce
das	Lebensmittelgeschäft, -e	grocer's, general food store
das	Wechselgeld	change

ESSENTIAL WORDS (masculine)

der	Ball, ⸚e	ball
der	Fußball, ⸚e	football
der	Fußballfan, -s	football supporter
der	Fußballspieler	footballer
der	Läufer	runner
der	Pass, ⸚e	pass
der	Radsport	cycling
der	Rollschuh, -e	roller skate
der	Schlittschuh, -e	ice skate
der	Spieler	player
der	Sport, -e	sport, game
der	Sportplatz, ⸚e	sports ground, playing field
der	Wintersport	winter sport(s)

ESSENTIAL WORDS (neuter)

das	Angeln	fishing, angling
das	Endspiel, -e	final(s)
das	Fitnesszentrum, -tren	health club
das	Freibad, ⸚er	open-air swimming pool
das	Hallenbad, ⸚er	indoor swimming pool
das	Hockey	hockey
das	Kricket	cricket
das	Laufen	running
das	Radfahren	cycling
das	Reiten	horse-riding
das	Rudern	rowing
das	Rugby	rugby
das	Schlittschuhlaufen	(ice) skating
das	Schwimmbad, ⸚er	swimming baths
das	Schwimmen	swimming
das	Spiel, -e	play; game, match
das	Squash	squash
das	Stadion, -ien	stadium
das	Tennis	tennis
das	Turnen	gymnastics

IMPORTANT WORDS (*masculine*)

der **Basketball, ⁻e**	basketball
der **Fußballplatz, ⁻e**	football pitch
der **Golfplatz, ⁻e**	golf course
der **Golfschläger**	golf club (*stick*)
der **Netzball, ⁻e**	netball
der **Platz, ⁻e**	ground, playing field
der **Pokal, -e**	cup
der **Profi, -s**	pro
der **Schläger**	racket/bat/club *etc*
der **Ski, -er**	ski
der **Teilnehmer**	participant
der **Tennisplatz, ⁻e**	tennis court
der **Volleyball, ⁻e**	volleyball
der **Zuschauer**	spectator

ESSENTIAL + IMPORTANT WORDS (*feminine*)

die **Angelrute, -n**	fishing rod
die **Bundesliga**	football league
die **Fußballelf, -en**	football team
die **Halbzeit, -en**	half (*of match*); half-time
die **Leichtathletik**	athletics
die **Mannschaft, -en**	team
die **Rennbahn, -en**	racecourse, track
die **Spielerin**	player
die **Spielhälfte, -n**	half (*of match*)
die **Turnhalle, -n**	gym(nasium)
die **Weltmeisterschaft, -en**	world championship(s)

USEFUL PHRASES

treibst du gern Sport? do you like sports?
spielen to play; laufen to run; werfen to throw;
springen to jump; trainieren to train; joggen to go jogging
üben to practise; trimmen to do exercises
gewinnen to win; verlieren to lose
unentschieden enden to end in a draw

IMPORTANT WORDS (neuter)

das	Billard	billiards
das	Boxen	boxing
das	Ergebnis, -se	result
das	Golf(spiel)	golf
das	Jogging	jogging
das	Netz, -e	net
das	Pferderennen	horse racing; horse-race
das	Rennen	racing, race meeting
das	Schießen	shooting
das	Segeln	sailing
das	Skateboard, -s	skateboard
das	Skifahren; das Skilaufen	skiing
das	Snowboard, -s	snowboard
das	Tauchen	(underwater) diving
das	Tischtennis	table tennis
das	Tor, -e	goal
das	Ziel, -e	goal, aim; finish, finishing post

USEFUL WORDS (neuter)

das	Bergsteigen	mountaineering
das	Bogenschießen	archery
das	gemischte Doppel	mixed doubles
das	Drachenfliegen	hang-gliding
das	Fechten	fencing
das	Gleitschirmfliegen	paragliding
das	Jagen	hunting; shooting
das	Klettern	climbing, mountaineering
die	Olympischen Spiele (pl)	Olympic Games
das	Ringen	wrestling
das	Surfbrett	surfboard
das	Tauziehen	tug-of-war
das	Training	training
das	Turnier, -e	tournament
das	Wasserski	water-skiing

USEFUL WORDS (masculine)

der	Bergsteiger	mountaineer
der	Federball, ̈-e	badminton; shuttlecock
der	Gegner	opponent
der	Hochsprung, ̈-e	high jump
der	Kampf, ̈-e	fight; contest
der	Meister	champion
der	Rodel	toboggan
der	Satz, ̈-e	set (tennis)
der	Schiedsrichter	referee; umpire
der	Schlitten	sledge, sleigh
der	Sieger	winner
der	Stoß, ̈-e	kick; push, thrust
der	Titelverteidiger	title-holder
der	Torwart, -e	goalkeeper
der	Trainer	trainer, coach; manager
die	Turnschuhe (pl)	tennis or gym shoes
	Unparteiische(r), -n	umpire; referee
der	Weitsprung, ̈-e	long jump
der	(Welt)rekord, -e	(world) record
der	Wettbewerb, -e	competition
der	Wettkampf, ̈-e	match, contest

USEFUL WORDS (feminine)

die	(Aschen)bahn, -en	(cinder) track
die	Bundesliga	national league
die	Eisbahn, -en	ice rink, skating rink
die	Kegelbahn, -en	bowling alley; skittle alley
die	Meisterschaft, -en	championship
die	Partie, -n	game, match
die	Punktzahl, -en	score
die	Runde, -n	lap, round
die	Siegerin	winner
die	Stoppuhr, -en	stopwatch
die	(Tabellen)spitze, -n	lead (in league etc)
die	Tribüne, -n	stand

ESSENTIAL WORDS *(masculine)*

der	**Ausgang, ⁝e**	exit, way out
der	**Eingang, ⁝e**	entrance, way in
der	**Film, -e**	film
der	**Kinobesucher**	cinema-goer
der	**Quatsch**	rubbish
der	**Theaterbesucher**	theatre-goer
die	**Zuhörer** *(pl)*	audience *(listeners)*

ESSENTIAL WORDS *(feminine)*

die	**Eintrittskarte, -n**	ticket
die	**Freizeit**	free *or* spare time
die	**Handlung, -en**	plot, action
die	**Kasse, -n**	box office, ticket office
die	**Musik**	music
die	**Reservierung, -en**	booking
die	**(Theater)karte, -n**	(theatre) ticket
die	**(Theater)kasse, -n**	box office
die	**Vorstellung, -en**	performance, show

ESSENTIAL WORDS *(neuter)*

das	**Kino, -s**	cinema
das	**Konzert, -e**	concert
das	**Spiel**	acting; play
das	**Theater**	theatre
das	**(Theater)stück, -e**	play

USEFUL PHRASES

ich gehe gern ins Kino/ins Theater I like going to the cinema/the theatre

an der Vorverkaufskasse at the booking office

„ausverkauft" "sold out"

mein Lieblingsfilmstar my favourite film star

ein Film mit Untertiteln a film with subtitles

spannend exciting; langweilig boring

(kaum) sehenswert (hardly) worth seeing

IMPORTANT WORDS (masculine)

der	Applaus, -e	applause
der	Balkon, -s or -e	(dress) circle
der	Bühneneingang, ⁝e	stage door
der	Dramatiker	dramatist, playwright
der	(Film)star, -s	(film) star
der	Komiker	comedian
der	Konzertsaal, -säle	concert hall
der	Krieg, -e	war
der	Krimi, -s	thriller
der	Kritiker	critic
der	Rang, ⁝e	circle (in theatre)
der	Saal, Säle	hall; room
der	Schauspieler	actor
der	(Sitz)platz, ⁝e	seat
der	Spaß	fun
der	Spielplan, ⁝e	programme
der	Text, -e	script
der	Titel	title
der	Untertitel	subtitle
der	Videoclip, -s	video clip
der	Vorhang, ⁝e	curtain
der	Western, -s	western
die	Zuschauer (pl)	audience (viewers)
der	erste Rang	dress circle
der	zweite Rang	upper circle

USEFUL PHRASES

die Bühne betreten to step onto the stage
meine Damen und Herren! ladies and gentlemen!
ein Stück geben to put on a play
mit X und Y in den Hauptrollen with X and Y in the main roles
klatschen to clap

IMPORTANT WORDS (feminine)

die	**Aufführung, -en**	performance
die	**Bühne, -n**	stage, platform
die	**Ermäßigung, -en**	reduction
die	**Figur, -en**	character
die	**Garderobe, -n**	cloakroom; wardrobe
die	**Hauptrolle, -n**	main role or part
die	**Komödie, -n**	comedy
die	**Oper, -n**	opera; opera house
die	**Reklame, -n**	advertisement
die	**Rolle, -n**	role, part
die	**Saison, -s**	season
die	**Schauspielerin**	actress
die	**Schlange, -n**	queue
die	**Seifenoper, -n**	soap opera
die	**Show, -s**	show
die	**Szene, -n**	scene
die	**Theatergruppe, -n**	dramatic society
die	**Tragödie, -n**	tragedy

IMPORTANT WORDS (neuter)

das	**Ballett, -e**	ballet
das	**Drama, Dramen**	drama
das	**Foyer, -s**	foyer
das	**Kostüm, -e**	costume
das	**Kriminalstück, -e**	thriller
das	**Make-up**	make-up
das	**Musical, -s**	musical
das	**Opernglas, ̈er**	(pair of) opera glasses
das	**Orchester**	orchestra; band
das	**Parkett, -e**	stalls (pl)
das	**Schauspiel, -e**	play
das	**Schauspielhaus, -häuser**	theatre

USEFUL WORDS *(masculine)*

der	Abgang, ⸚e	exit *(of actor)*
der	Auftritt, -e	entrance *(of actor)*; scene *(of play)*
der	Beifall	applause
der	Intendant, -en	stage manager
der	Orchesterraum, -räume	orchestra pit
der	Produzent, -en	(film) producer
der	Regisseur, -e	producer; director
der	Souffleur, -e	prompter
der	Spielfilm, -e	feature film
der	Western	western

USEFUL WORDS *(feminine)*

die	Farce, -n	farce
die	Galerie, -n	the "gods", gallery
die	Generalprobe, -n	dress rehearsal
die	Inszenierung, -en	production
die	Kapelle, -n	band
die	Kritik, -en	review
die	Leinwand, ⸚e	screen
die	Loge, -n	box
die	Pause, -n	interval
die	Platzanweiserin	usherette, attendant
die	Probe, -n	rehearsal
die	Schauspielkunst	acting
die	Souffleuse, -n	prompter
die	Tribüne, -n	platform
die	Zugabe, -n	encore

USEFUL WORDS *(neuter)*

das	Lustspiel, -e	comedy
das	Plakat, -e	poster, notice
das	Rampenlicht	footlights *(pl)*
das	Scheinwerferlicht, -er	spotlight
das	Trauerspiel, -e	tragedy

ESSENTIAL WORDS (*masculine*)

der	**Abend, -e**	evening
der	**Augenblick, -e**	moment, instant
der	**Beginn, -e**	beginning
der	**Mittag, -e**	mid-day, noon
der	**Moment, -e**	moment
der	**Monat, -e**	month
der	**Morgen**	morning
der	**Nachmittag, -e**	afternoon
der	**Tag, -e**	day
der	**Vormittag, -e**	morning
der	**Wecker**	alarm clock

ESSENTIAL WORDS (*feminine*)

die	**Armbanduhr, -en**	(wrist) watch
die	**Jahreszeit, -en**	season
die	**Minute, -n**	minute
die	**Mitte**	middle
die	**Mitternacht, ⁝e**	midnight
die	**Nacht, ⁝e**	night; night-time
die	**Sekunde, -n**	second
die	**halbe Stunde, -n -n**	half-hour, half-an-hour
die	**Stunde, -n**	hour
die	**Tageszeit, -en**	daytime
die	**Uhr, -en**	clock; time
die	**Viertelstunde, -n**	quarter of an hour
die	**Weile, -n**	while, short time
die	**Woche, -n**	week
die	**Zeit, -en**	time

ESSENTIAL WORDS (*neuter*)

das	**Datum, Daten**	date
das	**Ende, -n**	end
das	**Jahr, -e**	year
das	**Jahrhundert, -e**	century
das	**Mal, -e**	time, occasion
das	**Wochenende, -n**	weekend

USEFUL PHRASES

um 7 Uhr aufstehen to get up at 7 o'clock
um 11 Uhr zu Bett gehen to go to bed at 11 o'clock
wie viel Uhr ist es?, wie spät ist es? what time is it?
den Wievielten haben wir heute? what is today's date?
früh early; spät late; bald soon; später later
fast almost; pünktlich punctual
es ist gerade or Punkt 2 Uhr it is exactly 2 o'clock
halb 3 half past 2; halb 9 half past 8
gegen 8 Uhr round about 8 o'clock
es ist Viertel nach 5/Viertel vor 5 it is a quarter past 5/a quarter to 5

vorgestern	the day before yesterday
gestern	yesterday
am vorigen or vorhergehenden Tag	the day before, the previous day
heute	today
heute Abend	tonight
morgen	tomorrow
am nächsten or folgenden Tag	the next or following day
übermorgen	the day after tomorrow
am übernächsten Tag	two days later
vierzehn Tage	a fortnight

USEFUL PHRASES

morgens in the morning; nachmittags in the afternoon
abends in the evening; nachts at night, by night
tagsüber, am Tage during the day; stündlich hourly
täglich daily; wöchentlich weekly
monatlich monthly; jährlich annually; heutzutage nowadays

IMPORTANT WORDS *(feminine)*

die	**Essenszeit, -en**	mealtime
die	**Gelegenheit, -en**	opportunity, occasion
die	**Kuckucksuhr, -en**	cuckoo clock
die	**Uhrzeit, -en**	time of day

USEFUL PHRASES

einen Augenblick! just a minute!
in diesem/dem Augenblick at this/that moment
im selben Augenblick at that very moment
ich habe keine Zeit (dazu) I have no time (for it)
(sich) die Zeit vertreiben to pass the time
es ist Zeit zum Essen it is time for lunch (dinner etc)
eine Zeit lang bleiben to stay for a while
anderthalb Stunden warten to wait an hour and a half
damals at that time
nie, niemals never; jemals ever
diesmal this time; ein anderes Mal another time
nächstes Mal next time
das erste/letzte Mal the first/last time
zum ersten/letzten Mal for the first/last time
am Wochenende at the weekend
über das Wochenende for the weekend
ich habe es eilig I'm in a hurry
ich habe keine Eile I'm in no hurry
es hat keine Eile there's no hurry

USEFUL WORDS (masculine)

der	Einbruch der Nacht	nightfall
der	Kalender	calendar
der	Tagesanbruch	daybreak
der	(Uhr)zeiger	hand (of clock etc)
der	Zeitabschnitt, -e	time, period

USEFUL WORDS (feminine)

die	Epoche, -n	epoch, period
die	Gegenwart	present (time, tense)
die	Mittagszeit, -en	lunch time
die	Pause, -n	interval; pause, break
die	Standuhr, -en	grandfather clock
die	Stoppuhr, -en	stopwatch
die	Vergangenheit	past (time, tense)
die	Verspätung, -en	delay (of vehicle)
die	Zukunft	future (time, tense)

USEFUL WORDS (neuter)

das	Futur(um)	future tense
das	Jahrtausend, -e	millennium
das	Jahrzehnt, -e	decade
das	Mittelalter	the Middle Ages
das	Präsens	present tense
das	Schaltjahr, -e	leap year
das	Zeitalter	age, time
das	Zifferblatt, ̈-er	(clock) face, dial

USEFUL PHRASES

vor einer Woche/einem Monat/2 Jahren a week/a month/2 years ago
gestern/heute vor einer Woche a week ago yesterday/today
gestern/heute vor 2 Jahren 2 years ago yesterday/today
in einer Woche/einem Monat/2 Jahren in a week('s time)/a month('s time)/
   2 years(' time)
morgen/heute in einer Woche a week tomorrow/today

ESSENTIAL + IMPORTANT WORDS (*masculine*)

der Bastler	handyman
der Bohrer	drill
der Dosenöffner	tin-opener
der Hammer, ⁼	hammer
der Holzhammer, ⁼	mallet
der Klebstoff, -e	glue
der Korkenzieher	corkscrew
der Schlüssel	key

ESSENTIAL + IMPORTANT WORDS (*feminine*)

die Batterie, -n	battery
die Baustelle, -n	building site
die Gabel, -n	fork
die Maschine, -n	machine; engine
die Werkstatt, ⁼en	workshop

ESSENTIAL + IMPORTANT WORDS (*neuter*)

das Ding, -e	thing, object
das Do-it-yourself	do-it-yourself, D.I.Y.
das *or der* Gummi	rubber; gum
das Gummiband, ⁼er	rubber band; elastic
das Kabel	wire; cable
das Schloss, ⁼er	lock

USEFUL WORDS (*neuter*)

das Brett, -er	plank, board; shelf
das Gerüst, -e	scaffolding
das Seil, -e	rope, cable
das Tau, -e	rope
das Werkzeug, -e	tool

USEFUL PHRASES
basteln: er kann gut basteln he is good with his hands
wozu benutzt man ...? what do you use ... for?
reparieren to repair; etw reparieren lassen to have sth repaired
nageln to nail; sägen to saw

USEFUL WORDS *(masculine)*

der	**Bolzen**	bolt
der	**Büchsenöffner**	tin-opener
der	**Draht, ⸚e**	wire
der	**Flaschenöffner**	bottle-opener
der	**Hobel**	plane
der	**Kleb(e)streifen**	adhesive tape
der	**Meißel**	chisel
der	**Nagel, ⸚**	nail
der	**Pickel**	pick, pickaxe
der	**Pinsel**	paintbrush
der	**Pressluftbohrer**	pneumatic drill
der	**Schraubenschlüssel**	spanner
der	**Schraubenzieher**	screwdriver
der	**Schraubstock, ⸚e**	vice
der	**Stacheldraht, ⸚e**	barbed wire
der	**Stift, -e**	peg
der	**Tesafilm®**	Sellotape®
der	**Werkzeugkasten, ⸚**	toolbox

USEFUL WORDS *(feminine)*

die	**Feder, -n**	spring, coil
die	**Feile, -n**	file
die	**Heftzwecke, -n**	drawing pin, thumbtack
die	**Kelle, -n**	trowel
die	**Leiter, -n**	ladder
die	**Nadel, -n**	needle; pin
die	**Planke, -n**	plank
die	**Reißzwecke, -n**	drawing pin, thumbtack
die	**Säge, -n**	saw
die	**Schaufel**	shovel; scoop
die	**Schere, -n**	(pair of) scissors
die	**Schnur, ⸚e**	string, cord; wire, flex
die	**Schraube, -n**	screw
die	**Wasserwaage, -n**	spirit level
die	**Zange, -n**	(pair of) pliers

ESSENTIAL WORDS *(masculine)*

der	Bahnhof, ⸚e	railway station
der	Bürgersteig, -e	pavement
der	Busbahnhof, ⸚e	bus or coach station
der	Dom, -e	cathedral
der	Laden, ⸚	shop
der	Markt, ⸚e	market
der	Markttag, -e	market day
der	Park, -s	(public) park
der	Parkplatz, ⸚e	parking place; car park
der	Polizist, -en	policeman
der	Turm, ⸚e	tower
der	Weg, -e	way

ESSENTIAL WORDS *(feminine)*

die	Brücke, -n	bridge
die	Burg, -en	castle
die	Bushaltestelle, -n	bus stop
die	Ecke, -n	corner, turning
die	Einbahnstraße, -n	one-way street
die	Fabrik, -en	factory, works
die	Fahrt, -en	journey
die	Haltestelle, -n	(bus or tram) stop
die	Hauptstraße, -n	main road; main street
die	Innenstadt, ⸚e	city centre, town centre
die	Kirche, -n	church
die	Klinik, -en	hospital, clinic
die	Polizei	police
die	(Polizei)wache, -n	police station
die	Post, Postämter	post office
die	Reise, -n or die Rundfahrt, -en	tour
die	Stadt, ⸚e	town; city
die	Straße, -n	street, road
die	Straßenecke, -n	street corner
die	Tankstelle, -n	service station, garage
die	U-Bahn, -en	underground (railway)

ESSENTIAL WORDS *(neuter)*

das Büro, -s	office
das Geschäft, -e	shop
das Heft, -e	book *(of tickets)*
das Hotel, -s	hotel
das Kaufhaus, -häuser	department store
das Kino, -s	cinema
das Krankenhaus, -häuser	hospital
das Museum, Museen	museum
das Parken	parking
das Parkhaus, -häuser	(covered) car park
das Postamt, ˝er	post office
das Rathaus, -häuser	town hall
das Restaurant, -s	restaurant
das Schloss, ˝er	castle
das Stadtzentrum, -tren	city centre, town centre
das Straßenschild, -er	roadsign
das Taxi, -s	taxi
das Theater	theatre
das Verkehrsamt, ˝er	tourist information centre

USEFUL PHRASES

in die Stadt gehen *or* fahren **to go into town**
in der Stadtmitte **in the centre of town**
eine Stadtrundfahrt machen **to go on a tour of the city**
die Straße übergehen **to cross the road**
die Sehenswürdigkeiten besichtigen **to have a look at the sights**

IMPORTANT WORDS (masculine)

der Betrieb	bustle
der Bezirk, -e	district
der Biergarten, ⁻	beer garden
der Bürgermeister	mayor
der Einwohner	inhabitant
der Fahrscheinautomat, -en	ticket machine
der Fahrscheinentwerter	automatic ticket stamping machine
der Friedhof, ⁻e	cemetery, graveyard
der Fußgänger	pedestrian
der Kreisverkehr	roundabout
der Platz, ⁻e	square
der Verkehr	traffic
der Verkehrsstau, -e	traffic jam
der Zebrastreifen	zebra crossing

IMPORTANT WORDS (feminine)

die Aussicht, -en	view
die Bürgermeisterin	female mayor
die Feuerwehrwache, -n	fire station
die Fußgängerzone, -n	pedestrian precinct
die Menge, -n	crowd
die Schlange, -n	queue
die Sehenswürdigkeiten (pl)	sights, places of interest
die Umgebung, -en	the surroundings (pl)

IMPORTANT WORDS (neuter)

das Denkmal, ⁻er	monument
das Fahrzeug, -e	vehicle
das Gebäude	building
das Tor, -e	gate(way), arch

USEFUL WORDS (masculine)

der **Abwasserkanal, ⸚e**	sewer
der **Bürger**	citizen
der **Fußgängerüberweg, -e**	pedestrian crossing
der **Kinderwagen**	pram
der **Landkreis, -e**	(like British) county
der **Marktplatz, ⸚e**	market place
der **Ort, -e**	place, spot
der **Passant, -en**	passer-by
der **Pfad, -e**	path
der **Pflasterstein, -e**	paving stone
der **Rad(fahr)weg, -e**	cycle path or track
der **Stadtbewohner** or der **Städter**	town dweller
der **Stadtrand, ⸚er**	the outskirts (pl)
der **Straßenübergang, ⸚e**	pedestrian crossing
der **Taxistand, ⸚e**	taxi rank
der **Umzug, ⸚e**	parade
der **Wegweiser**	roadsign
der **Wohnblock, -s**	block of flats
der **Wolkenkratzer**	skyscraper

USEFUL PHRASES

in der Stadt/am Stadtrand wohnen to live in the town/in the suburbs
auf dem Platz in or on the square
an der Ecke at or on the corner
zum Markt gehen, auf den Markt gehen to go to the market
Weihnachtsmarkt Christmas fair
zu Fuß gehen to walk
mit dem Bus/mit dem Zug fahren to go by bus/by train
ein Taxi anrufen to call a taxi
ins Theater/ins Kino gehen to go to the theatre/the cinema
modern modern; alt old
sauber clean; schmutzig dirty
typisch typical; ziemlich quite; sehr very

USEFUL WORDS *(feminine)*

die	Altstadt	old (part of) town
die	Baustelle, -n	building site; roadworks
die	Bevölkerung, -en	population
die	Gasse, -n	lane, back street
die	Großstadt, ⁻e	city
die	Kreuzung, -en	crossroads
die	Kunstgalerie, -n	art gallery
die	Leuchtreklame, -n	neon sign
die	Meinungsumfrage, -n	opinion poll
die	Parkuhr, -en	parking meter
die	Prozession, -en	procession
die	Sackgasse, -n	dead end
die	Siedlung, -en	housing estate
die	Sozialwohnung, -en	council flat *or* house
die	Spitze, -n	spire
die	Stadtmitte, -n	town centre; city centre
die	Statue, -n	statue
die	Straßenbahn, -en	tram
die	Straßenlaterne, -n	street lamp
die	Tour, -en	tour
die	Umgehungsstraße, -n	by-pass
die	Umleitung, -en	diversion
die	Vorstadt, ⁻e	suburbs *(pl)*

USEFUL WORDS (neuter)

das	Gedränge	crowd
das	Industriegebiet, -e	industrial area
das	Kopfsteinpflaster	cobblestones
das	Plakat, -e	poster, notice
das	Schild, -er	sign
das	(Stadt)viertel	district
das	Werk, -e	factory, works
das	Wohngebiet, -e	built-up area
das	Zentrum, -tren	city centre

USEFUL PHRASES

„Betreten der Baustelle verboten" "building site: keep out"
„Anlieger frei" "residents only"
„Vorsicht, bissiger Hund!" "beware of the dog"
„Fußgängerzone" "pedestrian precinct"
„bitte frei halten" "please keep clear"
„Parken verboten" "no parking"
„Vorfahrt achten!" "give way"

ESSENTIAL WORDS (*masculine*)

der	**Ausgang, ¨e**	exit
der	**Ausstieg, -e**	exit (*from train*)
der	**Bahnhof, ¨e**	station
der	**Bahnsteig, -e**	platform
der	**D-Zug, ¨e** (*Durchgangszug*)	through train
der	**Eilzug, ¨e**	limited-stop train
der	**Eingang, ¨e**	entrance
der	**Einstieg, -e**	entrance (*onto train*)
der	**Entwerter**	ticket punching machine
der	**Fahrgast, ¨e**	passenger
der	**Fahrkartenschalter**	ticket *or* booking office
der	**Fahrschein, -e**	ticket
der	**Fahrplan, ¨e**	timetable
der	**Hauptbahnhof, ¨e**	main *or* central station
der	**Intercity(zug), -s/(¨e)**	inter-city train
der	**Koffer**	case, suitcase
der	**Kofferkuli, -s**	luggage trolley
der	**Nahverkehrszug, ¨e**	local train
der	**Passagier, -e**	passenger
	Reisende(r), -n	traveller
der	**Rucksack, ¨e**	rucksack, backpack
der	**Schnellimbiss, -e**	snack bar
der	**Schnellzug, ¨e**	fast train, express train
der	**Speisewagen**	dining car
der	**U-Bahnhof, ¨e**	underground station
der	**Wagen**	carriage, coach
der	**Zug, ¨e**	train
der	**Zuschlag, ¨e**	supplement

ESSENTIAL WORDS (*neuter*)

das	**Gepäck**	luggage
das	**Gleis, -e**	platform; track, rails
das	**Rad, ¨er**	bike
das	**Schließfach, ¨er**	left luggage locker
das	**Taxi, -s**	taxi

ESSENTIAL WORDS *(feminine)*

die Abfahrt, -en	departure
die Ankunft, ⸚e	arrival
die Auskunft, ⸚e	information; information desk *or* office
die Bahn, -en	railway
die Bahnlinie, -n	railway line
die Brücke, -n	bridge
Deutsche Bahn (DB)	German Railways
die Einfahrt, -en	entrance
die (einfache) Fahrkarte, (-n) -n	(single) ticket
die Fahrt, -en	journey
die Haltestelle, -n	stop, station
die Klasse, -n	class
die Linie, -n	line
die Reise, -n	journey
die Richtung, -en	direction
die Rückfahrkarte, -n	return ticket
die S-Bahn, -en	high-speed railway; suburban railway
die Station, -en	station
die Tasche, -n	bag
die U-Bahn, -en *(Untergrundbahn)*	underground (railway)
die U-Bahnstation, -en	underground station
die Uhr, -en	clock; time

USEFUL PHRASES

auf dem Bahnhof at the station
sich erkundigen to make inquiries
einen Platz reservieren to book a seat
nach Bonn einfach a single to Bonn
nach Bonn und zurück a return to Bonn
zweimal nach Bonn und zurück two returns to Bonn
für diese Züge muss man Zuschlag bezahlen you have to pay a supplement on these trains
„bitte einsteigen!" "all aboard"; „alles aussteigen!" "all change"
muss ich umsteigen? do I have to change trains?

IMPORTANT WORDS (masculine)

der	Anschluss, -̈e	connection
der	Dienst, -e	service
der	Dienstwagen	guard's van
der	Eisenbahner	railwayman
der	Fahrausweis, -e	ticket
der	Gepäckwagen	luggage van
der	ICE, -s or der Intercityexpress	high-speed inter-city (train)
der	Liegewagen	couchette
der	Lokomotivführer	train driver
der	Platz, -̈e	seat
der	Schaffner	guard; ticket collector
der	Schlafwagen	sleeping car, sleeper
der	Zollbeamte, -n	customs officer

IMPORTANT WORDS (feminine)

die	Bahnhofsgaststätte, -n	station buffet
die	Bremse, -n	brake
die	Eisenbahn, -en	railway
die	Gepäckaufbewahrung, -en	left luggage office
die	Grenze, -n	border, frontier
die	Mehrfahrtenkarte,-n	season ticket
die	Notbremse, -n	alarm, communication cord
die	Verbindung, -en	connection
die	Verspätung, -en	delay
die	Zollkontrolle, -n	customs control or check

IMPORTANT WORDS (neuter)

das	Abteil, -e	compartment
das	Fahrgeld, -er	fare
das	Gepäcknetz, -e	luggage rack
das	Nichtraucherabteil, -e	non-smoking compartment
das	Raucherabteil, -e	smoking compartment
das	(Reise)ziel, -e	destination

USEFUL WORDS (masculine)

der	Anhänger	label, tag
der	Bahnübergang, ⁻e	level crossing
der	Bestimmungsort, -e	destination (of goods)
der	Fahrpreis, -e	fare
der	Gepäckträger	porter
der	Güterzug, ⁻e	goods train
der	Personenzug, ⁻e	slow train; passenger train
der	Pfiff, -e	whistle
der	Schrankkoffer	trunk
der	Taxistand, ⁻e	taxi rank
der	Vorortzug, ⁻e	commuter train
der	Wartesaal, -säle	waiting room

USEFUL WORDS (feminine)

die	Bahncard, -s	railcard
die	(Eisenbahn)schienen (pl)	rails
die	Endstation, -en	terminus
die	Entgleisung, -en	derailment
die	Lokomotive, -n	locomotive, engine
die	Monatskarte, -n	monthly season ticket
die	Nummer, -n	number
die	Reservierung, -en	reservation
die	Rolltreppe, -n	escalator
die	Schienen (pl)	rails
die	Schranke, -n	level crossing gate
die	Sperre, -n	barrier
die	Strecke, -n	(section of) railway line or track
die	Wochenkarte, -n	weekly ticket

USEFUL PHRASES

mit der Bahn by rail
den Zug erreichen/verpassen to catch/miss one's train
ist dieser Platz frei? is this seat free?
hier ist besetzt this seat is taken
„nicht hinauslehnen" "do not lean out of the window"
verspätet delayed

USEFUL WORDS (feminine)

die	**Beere, -n**	berry
die	**Birke, -n**	birch
die	**Blutbuche, -n**	copper beech
die	**Buche, -n**	beech tree
die	**Eibe, -n**	yew
die	**Eiche, -n**	oak
die	**Esche, -n**	ash
die	**Fichte, -n**	spruce, pine
die	**Föhre, -n**	Scots pine
die	**Kastanie, -n**	chestnut; chestnut tree
die	**Kiefer, -n**	pine
die	**Knospe, -n**	bud
die	**Linde, -n**	lime tree
die	**Mistel, -n**	mistletoe
die	**Pappel, -n**	poplar
die	**Pinie, -n**	pine
die	**Platane, -n**	plane tree
die	**Rinde, -n**	bark
die	**Rosskastanie, -n**	horse chestnut
die	**Stechpalme, -n**	holly
die	**Tanne, -n**	fir tree
die	**Trauerweide, -n**	weeping willow
die	**Ulme, -n**	elm
die	**Weide, -n**	willow
die	**Wurzel, -n**	root

IMPORTANT + USEFUL WORDS (neuter)

das	**Blatt, ¨er**	leaf
das	**Geäst** (sg)	branches
das	**Gebüsch** (sg)	bushes; undergrowth
das	**Holz, ¨er**	wood (material)

USEFUL PHRASES

auf einen Baum klettern to climb a tree
im Herbst werden die Blätter gelb the leaves turn yellow in autumn
im Schatten eines Baums in the shade of a tree

ESSENTIAL + IMPORTANT WORDS (masculine)

der **Baum, Bäume**	tree
der **Christbaum, -bäume**	Christmas tree
der **Forst, -e**	forest
der **Obstbaum, -bäume**	fruit tree
der **Obstgarten,** ⸚	orchard
der **Schatten**	shade, shadow
der **Wald,** ⸚**er**	wood(s), forest
der **Weihnachtsbaum, -bäume**	Christmas tree

USEFUL WORDS (masculine)

der **Ahorn, -e**	maple
der **Ast,** ⸚**e**	branch
der **Buchsbaum, -bäume**	box tree
der **Busch,** ⸚**e**	bush, shrub
der **Eich(en)baum, -bäume**	oak tree
der **Kastanienbaum, -bäume**	chestnut tree
der **Kiefernzapfen**	pine cone
der **Mistelzweig, -e**	(sprig of) mistletoe
der **Rotdorn, -e**	hawthorn
der **Stamm,** ⸚**e**	trunk
der **Strauch, Sträucher**	bush, shrub
der **Tannenbaum, -bäume**	fir tree
der **Tannenzapfen**	fir cone
der **Weidenbaum, -bäume**	willow
der **Weinberg, -e**	vineyard
der **Wipfel**	tree-top
der **Zweig, -e**	branch

ESSENTIAL WORDS (masculine)

der	Champignon, -s	(button) mushroom
der	Kohl, -e	cabbage
der	Kopfsalat, -e	lettuce
der	Salat, -e	lettuce; salad

IMPORTANT WORDS (masculine)

der	Blumenkohl, -e	cauliflower
der	Knoblauch	garlic
der	Pilz, -e	mushroom
der	Rosenkohl	Brussels sprouts (pl)
der	Vegetarier	vegetarian

USEFUL WORDS (masculine)

der	Gartenkürbis, -se	marrow
der	Kürbis, -se	pumpkin
der	Lauch, -e	leek
der	Mais	sweetcorn
der	Maiskolben	corn on the cob
der	(rote/grüne) Paprika, (-n) -s	(red/green) pepper
der	Porree, -s	leek
der	Rettich, -e	(large) radish
der	Rotkohl, -e	red cabbage
der	or die Sellerie	celeriac; celery
der	Spargel	asparagus
der	Spinat	spinach
der	or die Stangensellerie	celery
der	Weißkohl, -e	white cabbage

USEFUL PHRASES

Gemüse anbauen to grow vegetables; organisch organic
Salzkartoffeln (pl) boiled potatoes
Pellkartoffeln (pl) potatoes boiled in their jackets
Bratkartoffeln (pl) fried or sauté potatoes
Knoblauchwurst (f) garlic sausage
geraspelte Möhre grated carrot
rot wie eine Tomate as red as a beetroot
vegetarisch vegetarian

ESSENTIAL WORDS (feminine)

die	Bohne, -n	bean
die	grüne Bohne, -n -n	French bean
die	Erbse, -n	pea
die	Kartoffel, -n	potato
die	Tomate, -n	tomato
die	Zwiebel, -n	onion

IMPORTANT WORDS (feminine)

die	Aubergine, -n	aubergine
die	Avocado, -s	avocado (pear)
die	Brokkoli (pl)	broccoli
die	Gurke, -n	cucumber
die	Karotte, -n	carrot
die	Vegetarierin	vegetarian

USEFUL WORDS (feminine)

die	Artischocke, -n	artichoke
die	Aubergine, -n	aubergine
die	Brunnenkresse	watercress
die	Endivie, -n	endive
die	Erdartischocke, -n	Jerusalem artichoke
die	Essiggurke, -n	gherkin
die	Kresse	cress
die	Möhre, -n; die Mohrrübe, -n	carrot
die	Paprikaschote, -n	pepper, capsicum
die	Pastinake, -n	parsnip
die	Petersilie	parsley
die	Rübe, -n	turnip
die	Rote Bete or Rübe, -n -n	beetroot
die	Zucchini	courgette

ESSENTIAL + IMPORTANT WORDS (neuter)

das	Gemüse	vegetable(s)
das	Kraut, Kräuter	herb; cabbage
das	Radieschen	radish
das	Sauerkraut	pickled cabbage

ESSENTIAL WORDS (*masculine*)

der **Bus, -se**	bus
der **Dampfer**	steamer
der **Krankenwagen**	ambulance
der **Lastkraftwagen (Lkw)**	lorry, truck; heavy goods vehicle
der **Personenkraftwagen (Pkw)**	private car
der **Polizeiwagen**	police car
der **Straßenbahnwagen**	tramcar
der **Tanker**	tanker
der **Wagen**	car; cart; carriage
der **Wohnwagen**	caravan
der **Zug, ̈-e**	train

ESSENTIAL WORDS (*feminine*)

die **Fähre, -n**	ferry
die **Straßenbahn, -en**	tram
die **U-Bahn, -en**	underground

ESSENTIAL WORDS (*neuter*)

das **Auto, -s**	car
das **Boot, -e**	boat
das **Fährboot, -e**	ferry-boat
das **Fahrrad, ̈-er**	bicycle
das **Flugzeug, -e**	plane, aeroplane
das **Mofa, -s**	moped (*small*)
das **Motorboot, -e**	motorboat
das **Motorrad, ̈-er**	motorbike, motorcycle
das **Rad, ̈-er**	bike
das **Ruderboot, -e**	rowing boat
das **Schiff, -e**	ship, vessel
das **Taxi, -s**	taxi
das **Wohnmobil, -e**	camper, motor caravan

USEFUL PHRASES

reisen to travel
fahren to go
eine Reise machen to go on a journey
gute Reise! have a good trip!
mit der Bahn *or* dem Zug fahren to go by rail *or* by train
mit dem Auto fahren to drive, go by car
nach Frankfurt fliegen to fly to Frankfurt
zu Fuß gehen to walk, go on foot
trampen, per Anhalter fahren to hitch-hike
mit einer Höchstgeschwindigkeit von 100 Kilometern pro Stunde fahren
   to drive at a maximum speed of 100 kilometres per hour
seine Fahrkarte entwerten to cancel one's ticket (in machine)
Gebrauchtwagen second-hand cars
mieten to hire
ein Mietauto *(nt)* a hired car
öffentliche Verkehrsmittel *(pl)* public transport

IMPORTANT WORDS (masculine)

der	Bulldozer	bulldozer
der	Fahrpreis, -e	fare
der	Feuerwehrwagen	fire engine
der	Flugzeugträger	aircraft carrier
der	Hubschrauber	helicopter
der	Jeep, -s	jeep
der	Kindersportwagen	baby buggy, push-chair
der	Lieferwagen	van; delivery van
der	Möbelwagen	removal van, furniture van
der	(Motor)roller	(motor) scooter
der	(Reise)bus, -se	coach
der	Rücksitz, -e	back seat
der	Transporter	van; transporter
der	Vordersitz, -e	front seat

IMPORTANT WORDS (feminine)

die	Autofähre, -n	car ferry
die	fliegende Untertasse, -n -n	flying saucer
die	Gefahr, -en	danger, risk
die	Lokomotive, -n	locomotive, engine

IMPORTANT WORDS (neuter)

das	Fahrgeld, -er	fare
das	Fahrzeug, -e	vehicle
das	Feuerwehrauto, -s	fire engine
das	Kanu, -s	canoe
das	Moped, -s	moped
das	Raumschiff, -e	spaceship
das	Rettungsboot, -e	lifeboat
das	Schnellboot, -e	speedboat
das	Segelboot, -e	sailing boat
das	UFO, -s	UFO (unidentified flying object)

USEFUL WORDS (*masculine*)

der **Anhänger**	trailer
der **Karren**	cart
der **Kinderwagen**	pram
der **Kombiwagen**	estate car, station wagon
der **Lastkahn, ⁻e**	barge
der **(Luft)ballon, -s** *or* **-e**	balloon
der **Omnibus, -se**	bus
der **Panzer**	tank
der **Sattelschlepper**	articulated lorry
der **Schleppdampfer; der Schlepper**	tug, tugboat
der **Sessellift, -e** *or* **-s**	chairlift
der **Streifenwagen**	(police) patrol car
der **Vergnügungsdampfer**	pleasure steamer

USEFUL WORDS (*feminine*)

die **Dampfwalze, -n**	steamroller
die **Drahtseilbahn, -en**	cable railway, funicular
die **Düse, -n**	jet (plane)
die **Jacht, -en**	yacht
die **Planierraupe, -n**	bulldozer
die **Rakete, -n**	rocket
die **Schwebebahn, -en**	cable *or* overhead railway

USEFUL WORDS (*neuter*)

das **Düsenflugzeug, -e**	jet plane
das **Luftkissenboot, -e**	hovercraft
das **Paddelboot, -e**	canoe
das **Schlauchboot, -e**	inflatable dinghy
das **Segelflugzeug, -e**	glider
das **Tankschiff, -e**	tanker
das **Transportmittel**	means of transport (*goods*)
das **U-Boot, -e** (*Unterseeboot*)	submarine
das **Verkehrsmittel**	means of transport (*passengers*)

ESSENTIAL WORDS (*masculine*)

der	**Abend, -e**	evening
der	**Berg, -e**	mountain
der	**Blitz, -e**	(flash of) lightning
der	**Donner**	thunder
der	**Frost, ⁻e**	frost
der	**Frühling, -e**	spring
der	**Grad, -e**	degree
der	**Herbst, -e**	autumn
der	**Himmel**	sky; heaven
der	**Monat, -e**	month
der	**Morgen**	morning
der	**Nachmittag, -e**	afternoon
der	**Nebel**	fog, mist
der	**Nord(en)**	north
der	**Ort, -e** *or* ⁻**er**	place
der	**Osten**	east
der	**Regen**	rain
der	**Schnee**	snow
der	**Schneesturm, ⁻e**	snowstorm
der	**Sommer**	summer
der	**Sonnenschein**	sunshine
der	**Sturm, ⁻e**	storm, gale; tempest
der	**Süden**	south
der	**Westen**	west
der	**Wind, -e**	wind
der	**Winter**	winter

USEFUL PHRASES

blitzen to flash (es blitzt); donnern to thunder (es donnert)
frieren to freeze (es friert); gießen to pour (es gießt)
nieseln to drizzle (es nieselt); regnen to rain (es regnet)
scheinen to shine (die Sonne scheint)
schneien to snow (es schneit)
es fängt an zu schneien it's beginning to snow

ESSENTIAL WORDS (feminine)

die **Insel, -n**	island
die **Jahreszeit, -en**	season
die **Luft**	air
die **Nacht, ⸚e**	night
die **Natur**	nature
die **Sonne**	sun
die **Temperatur, -en**	temperature
die **Welt**	world
die **Wolke, -n**	cloud

ESSENTIAL WORDS (neuter)

das **Eis**	ice
das **Gewitter**	thunderstorm
das **Glatteis**	black ice
das **Jahr, -e**	year
das **Land, ⸚er**	country
das **Licht, -er**	light
das **Wetter**	weather

USEFUL PHRASES

wie ist das Wetter heute? what's the weather like today?

wie ist das Wetter bei euch? what's the weather like with you?

wie ist die Wettervorhersage? what's the weather forecast?

heiß hot; kalt cold

warm warm; kühl cool

herrlich marvellous; schön lovely; schrecklich terrible

sonnig sunny; windig windy

mild mild; rau harsh

schwül sultry, close; trüb dull

bedeckt overcast; bewölkt cloudy

stürmisch stormy; neblig misty

trocken dry; nass wet; feucht damp

heiter bright; regnerisch rainy

IMPORTANT WORDS (*masculine*)

der	Donnerschlag, ⸚e	thunderclap
der	Hagel	hail
der	Mond	moon
der	Mondschein	moonlight
der	Niederschlag, ⸚e	rainfall, precipitation
der	Planet, -en	planet
der	Regenschauer	shower of rain
der	(Regen)schirm, -e	umbrella
der	Regentropfen	raindrop
der	Schatten	shadow; shade
der	Schauer	shower
der	Schneefall, ⸚e	snowfall
der	Schneeregen	sleet
der	Smog	smog
der	Sonnenschirm, -e	parasol, sunshade
der	Stern, -e	star
der	Wetterbericht, -e	weather report

IMPORTANT WORDS (*feminine*)

die	Front, -en	front
die	Hitze	heat
die	Kälte	cold
die	Verbesserung, -en	improvement
die	Wetterlage	weather situation
die	Wettervorhersage,-n	weather forecast

IMPORTANT WORDS (*neuter*)

das	Halbdunkel	semi-darkness
das	Klima, -s *or* -ta	climate
das	Mondlicht	moonlight
das	Sauwetter	awful weather

USEFUL PHRASES
herrschen to prevail; zeitweise for a time
vereinzelt bewölkt with (occasional) cloudy patches
plus plus; minus minus
so ein Sauwetter! what awful weather!

USEFUL WORDS (masculine)

der	**Blitzableiter**	lightning conductor
der	**Dunst**	haze
der	**Eiszapfen**	icicle
der	**Gefrierpunkt**	freezing point
der	**Hochdruck**	high pressure
der	**Orkan, ⁻e**	hurricane
der	**Platzregen**	downpour
der	**Regenbogen**	rainbow
der	**Sonnenaufgang, ⁻e**	sunrise
der	**Sonnenstrahl, -en**	ray of sunshine
der	**Sonnenuntergang, ⁻e**	sunset
der	**Tagesanbruch**	dawn, break of day
der	**Tau**	dew
der	**Tiefdruck**	low pressure
der	**Windstoß, ⁻e**	gust of wind

USEFUL WORDS (feminine)

die	**Atmosphäre**	atmosphere
die	**Aufheiterungen** (pl)	bright periods
die	**Bö, -en**	squall, gust of wind
die	**Brise, -n**	breeze
die	**Dürre, -n**	(period of) drought
die	**Flut, -en**	flood
die	**Hitzewelle, -n**	heat wave
die	**Kältewelle, -n**	cold spell
die	**(Morgen)dämmerung, -en**	dawn
die	**Schneeflocke, -n**	snowflake
die	**Schneewehe, -n**	snowdrift
die	**Überschwemmung, -en**	flood, deluge

USEFUL WORDS (neuter)

das	**Barometer**	barometer
das	**Schneegestöber**	flurry of snow
das	**Tauwetter**	thaw
das	**Unwetter**	thunderstorm
das	**Zwielicht**	twilight

ESSENTIAL WORDS (*masculine*)

der	**Ausweis, -e**	card
der	**Empfang, ⸚e**	reception
der	**Herbergsvater, ⸚**	warden
der	**Junge, -n**	boy
der	**Rucksack, ⸚e**	backpack, rucksack
der	**Schlafsack, ⸚e**	sleeping bag
der	**Spaziergang, ⸚e**	walk
der	**Speisesaal, -säle**	dining room
der	**Stadtplan, ⸚e**	street map
der	**Urlaub, -e**	holiday(s)

ESSENTIAL WORDS (*feminine*)

die	**Anmeldung, -en**	registration
die	**Dusche, -n**	shower
die	**Herbergsmutter, ⸚**	(female) warden
die	**Jugendherberge, -n**	youth hostel
die	**Küche, -n**	kitchen
die	**Landkarte, -n**	map
die	**Mahlzeit, -en**	meal
die	**Toilette, -n**	toilet
die	**Übernachtung, -en**	overnight stay

ESSENTIAL WORDS (*neuter*)

das	**Abendessen**	dinner, evening meal
das	**Badezimmer**	bathroom
das	**Bett, -en**	bed
das	**Büro, -s**	office
das	**Essen**	food; meal
das	**Frühstück, -e**	breakfast
das	**Mädchen**	girl

USEFUL PHRASES

bleiben to stay
übernachten to spend the night
sich anmelden to register
mieten to hire
„Hausordnung für Jugendherbergen" "youth hostel rules"

IMPORTANT WORDS (masculine)

der	Aufenthalt, -e	stay
	Erwachsene(r), -n	adult
der	Feuerlöscher	fire extinguisher
	Jugendliche(r), -n	young person
der	Mülleimer	dustbin
der	Prospekt, -e	leaflet, brochure
der	Reiseführer	guidebook
der	Schlafsaal, -säle	dormitory
der	Waschraum, -räume	washroom
der	Waschsalon, -s	laundrette
der	Zimmernachweis, -e	accommodation office

IMPORTANT WORDS (feminine)

die	Bettwäsche	bed linen, bedclothes (pl)
die	Mitgliedskarte, -n	membership card
die	Nachtruhe	lights-out
die	Ruhe	quiet
die	Unterkunft, -künfte	accommodation
die	Veranstaltung, -en	organization
die	Wäsche	washing (things)

IMPORTANT WORDS (neuter)

das	Etagenbett, -en	bunk bed
das	Schwarze Brett, -n -er	notice board

The vocabulary items on pages 206 to 229 have been grouped under parts of speech rather than topics because they can apply in a wide range of circumstances. Use them just as freely as the vocabulary already given.

ADJECTIVES

What is an adjective?
An **adjective** is a 'describing' word that tells you more about a person or thing, such as their appearance, colour, size or other qualities, for example, *pretty*, *blue*, *big*.

abgenutzt worn out (*object*)
abscheulich hideous
ähnlich (*+ dat*) similar (to), like
aktuell topical
albern silly, foolish
allerlei all kinds of
allgemein general
alltäglich ordinary; daily
alt old
amüsant amusing
andere(r, s) other
anders different
angenehm pleasant
angrenzend neighbouring
arm poor
artig well-behaved, good
aufgeregt excited
aufgeweckt bright, lively
aufrichtig sincere
ausführlich detailed, elaborate
ausgestreckt stretched (out)
ausgezeichnet excellent
ausschließlich sole, exclusive
außerordentlich extra-ordinary
befriedigend satisfactory
begeistert keen, enthusiastic
belebt busy (*street*)

beleuchtet illuminated
beliebt popular
bemerkenswert remarkable
benachbart neighbouring
bereit ready
berühmt famous
beschäftigt (mit) busy (with) (*of person*)
besetzt engaged; taken
besondere(r, s) special
besorgt worried, anxious
besser better
betrunken drunk
beunruhigt worried, disturbed
blöd silly, stupid
brav well-behaved
breit wide, broad
bunt colourful
dankbar grateful
dauernd perpetual, constant
delikat delicate; delicious
deutlich clear; distinct
dicht thick, dense
dick thick
doof daft, stupid
dreckig dirty, filthy
dringend urgent

dumm silly, stupid; annoying
dunkel dark
dünn thin
dynamisch dynamic
echt real, genuine
ehemalig old, former
ehrlich sincere, honest
eifrig keen, enthusiastic
eigen own
einfach simple; single
einzeln single, individual
einzig only
elegant elegant, smart
elektrisch, Elektro- electric
elend poor, wretched
End- final
endgültig final, definite
endlos endless
eng narrow; tight
entschlossen firm, determined
entsetzlich dreadful
entzückend delightful
erfahren experienced
ernst serious, solemn
ernsthaft serious, earnest
erreichbar reachable, within reach
erschöpft exhausted, worn out
erste(r, s) first
erstaunlich amazing, extraordinary
erstaunt astonished
fähig (zu) capable (of)
falsch false; wrong
faul rotten; lazy
feierlich solemn
fein fine
fern far-off, distant
fertig prepared, ready
fest firm, hard

fett fat; greasy
finster dark
flach flat
fortgeschritten advanced
fortwährend continual, endless
frech cheeky
frei free, vacant
frisch fresh
furchtbar frightful
fürchterlich terrible, awful
ganz whole, complete
geduldig patient
geeignet suitable
gefährlich dangerous
gefroren frozen
geheim secret
geheimnisvoll mysterious
gemischt mixed
gemütlich comfortable
genau exact, precise
gerade straight; even
geringste(r, s) slightest, least
gesamt whole, entire
geschichtlich historical
gestattet allowed
gewaltig tremendous, huge
gewalttätig violent
gewiss certain
gewöhnlich usual; ordinary; common
glatt smooth
gleich same; equal
glücklich happy; fortunate
gnädig gracious
gnädige Frau Madam
graziös graceful
grob coarse, rude
groß big, great, large; tall
großartig magnificent

günstig suitable, convenient
gut good
hart hard
hässlich ugly
Haupt- main
heftig fierce, violent
heiß hot
hell pale; bright, light
herrlich marvellous
hervorragend excellent
historisch historical
hoch high
höflich polite, civil
hübsch pretty
intelligent intelligent
interessant interesting
jede(r, s) each, every
jung young
kalt cold
kein no, not any
klar clear, sharp
klatschnass soaking wet
klein small, little
klug wise, clever
komisch funny
kompliziert complicated
körperlich physical
kostbar expensive; precious
kostenlos free (of charge)
köstlich delicious
kräftig strong
kühl cool
kurz short
lächelnd smiling
lächerlich ridiculous
lahm lame
Landes- national
lang long; tall (of person)
langsam slow

langweilig boring
laut loud, noisy
lebendig alive; lively
lebhaft lively (of person)
lecker delicious, tasty
leer empty
leicht easy; light (weight)
leidenschaftlich passionate
leise quiet; soft
letzte(r, s) last, latest; final
lieb dear
Lieblings- favourite
linke(r, s) left
lustig amusing; cheerful
sich lustig machen über (+ acc)
  to make fun of
luxuriös luxurious
Luxus- luxury, luxurious
mächtig powerful, mighty
mager thin
mehrere several
merkwürdig strange, odd
Militär-, militärisch military
mindeste(r, s) least
mitleidig sympathetic
modern modern
möglich possible
müde tired
munter lively
mutig courageous
mysteriös mysterious
nächste(r, s) next; nearest
nah(e) near; close
natürlich natural
nett nice, kind
neu new
neugierig curious
niedrig low
nötig necessary

notwendig necessary
nützlich useful
nutzlos useless
obligatorisch compulsory, obligatory
offen open; frank, sincere
offenbar, offensichtlich obvious
öffentlich public
offiziell official
ordentlich (neat and) tidy
Orts- local
pädagogisch educational
passend suitable
persönlich personal
populär popular
prächtig magnificent
privat private; personal
privilegiert privileged
pünktlich punctual
Quadrat-, quadratisch square
rau rough; harsh
rechte(r, s) right
reich rich
reif ripe
rein clean
reizend charming
religiös religious
reserviert reserved
richtig right, correct
riesig huge, gigantic
romantisch romantic
ruhig quiet, peaceful
rund round
sanft gentle, soft
satt full (*person*)
ich habe es satt I'm fed up (with it)
sauber clean
scharf sharp; spicy
schattig shady

scheu shy
schick smart, chic
schläfrig sleepy
schlank slender, slim
schlau cunning, sly
schlecht bad
schlimm bad
schmal narrow; slender
schmutzig dirty
schnell fast, quick, rapid
schön beautiful
schrecklich terrible; frightful
schroff steep; jagged; brusque
schüchtern shy
schwach weak
schweigsam silent
schwer heavy; serious
schwierig difficult
seltsam strange, odd, curious
sicher sure; safe
sichtbar visible
solche(r, s) such
Sonder- special
sonderbar strange, odd
sorgenfrei carefree
sorgfältig careful
spannend exciting
Stadt-, städtisch municipal, urban
ständig perpetual
stark strong; heavy
steif stiff
steil steep
still quiet, still
stolz (auf + *acc*) proud (of)
streng severe, harsh; strict
stur stubborn
süß sweet
sympathisch likeable
tapfer brave

technisch technical
tief deep
toll mad; terrific
tot dead
tragbar portable
traurig sad
treu true (friend etc)
trocken dry
typisch typical
übel wicked, bad
übrig left-over
unartig naughty
unbekannt unknown
uneben uneven
unerträglich unbearable
ungeheuer huge
ungezogen rude
unglaublich incredible
unglücklich unhappy; unfortunate
unheimlich weird
unmöglich impossible
ursprünglich original
verantwortlich responsible
verboten prohibited, forbidden
verlegen embarrassed
verletzt injured
verliebt in love

vernünftig sensible, reasonable
verrückt mad, crazy
verschieden various; different
verständlich understandable
viereckig square
volkstümlich popular (of the people)
voll (+ gen) full (of)
vollkommen perfect, complete
vollständig complete
vorderste(r, s) front (row etc)
wach awake
wahr true
warm warm
weich soft
weise wise
weit wide
wert worth
wichtig important
wild fierce, wild
wohlhabend well-off
wunderbar wonderful, marvellous
zäh tough
zahlreich numerous
zart gentle, tender
zig umpteen
zufrieden satisfied, contented
zusätzlich extra

ADVERBS

What is an adverb?
An **adverb** is a word usually used with verbs, adjectives or other adverbs that gives more information about when, how, where, or in what circumstances something happens: *quickly, happily, now* are all adverbs.

Many other adverbs have the same form as the adjective.

absichtlich deliberately, on purpose
allein alone, on one's own some day
allerdings certainly; of course, to be sure
am besten best, best of all
am liebsten most (of all), best (of all)
am meisten (the) most
anders otherwise; differently
auf einmal all at once
äußerst extremely, most
bald soon; almost
besonders especially, particularly
bestimmt definitely, for sure
bloß only, merely
da there; here; then
daher from there; from that
dahin (to) there; then
damals at that time
danach after that; afterwards
dann then
darin in it, in there
deshalb therefore, for that reason
doch after all
dort there
dorthin (to) there
draußen out of doors; outside
drinnen inside; indoors
drüben over there, on the other side

durchaus thoroughly, absolutely
eben exactly; just
eher sooner; rather
eigentlich really, actually
einmal once; one day,
endlich at last, finally
erst first; only (*time*)
erstens first(ly), in the first place
etwa about; perhaps
fast almost, nearly
früh early
ganz quite; completely
gar nicht not at all
gegenwärtig at present, at the moment
genau exactly, precisely
genug enough
gerade just, exactly
geradeaus straight ahead
gern(e) willingly; gladly
gewöhnlich usually
glücklicherweise fortunately
gut well
häufig frequently
heutzutage nowadays
hier here
hierher this way, here
hin und her to and fro
hinten at the back, behind

höchst highly, extremely
hoffentlich I hope, hopefully
immer always
immer noch still
inzwischen meanwhile, in the meantime
irgendwo(hin) (to) somewhere
je ... desto: je mehr desto besser the more the better
je ever
jedenfalls in any case
jedesmal each time, everytime
jedesmal wenn whenever
jemals ever; at any time
jetzt now
kaum hardly, scarcely
keineswegs in no way; by no means
komischerweise funnily (enough), in a funny way
künftig in future
lange for a long time
langsam slowly
lauter *(with pl)* nothing but, only
leider unfortunately
lieber rather, preferably
links left; on *or* to the left
manchmal sometimes
mehr more
meinetwegen for my sake; on my account
meistens mostly, for the most part
mitten (in) in the middle *or* midst (of)
möglichst as ... as possible
nachher afterwards
natürlich naturally
neu füllen *etc* to refill *etc*
neu newly; afresh, anew

nicht not
nichtsdestoweniger nevertheless
nie, niemals never
noch einmal (once) again
noch still; yet
normalerweise normally
nun now
nur just, only
oben above; upstairs
oft often
plötzlich suddenly
rechts right; on *or* to the right
richtig correctly; really
rundherum round about, all (a)round
schlecht badly
schließlich finally
schnell quickly
schon already
sehr very, a lot, very much
selbst even
selten seldom, rarely
so so, thus, like this
sofort at once, immediately
sogar even
sogleich at once, straight away
sonst otherwise; or else
spät late
überall(hin) everywhere
übrigens besides, by the way
umher about, around
ungefähr about, approximately
unten below; downstairs; at the bottom
unterwegs on the way
viel much, a lot
vielleicht perhaps, maybe
völlig completely
vorbei by, past

vorher before, previously, beforehand
wahrscheinlich probably
wann(?) when(?)
warum(?) why(?)
weit far
wie(?), wie! how(?), how!
wieder again
wirklich really
wo/woher/wohin/wovon(?) where/from where/(to) where/from where(?)

ziemlich fairly, rather
zu to
zuerst first; at first
zufällig by chance; by any chance
zurück back
zweitens second(ly), in the second place

SOME MORE NOUNS

What is a noun?
A **noun** is a 'naming' word for a living being, thing or idea, for example, *woman, Andrew, desk, happiness.*

das Abenteuer adventure
der Abhang, ⁻e slope
die Abkürzung, -en abbreviation;
  short-cut
der Abschnitt, -e section
die Absicht, -en intention
der Abstieg, -e descent
die Abteilung, -en department,
  section
die Abwesenheit, -en absence
die Ahnung, -en idea, suspicion
die Änderung, -en alteration, change
der Anfang, ⁻e beginning
zu Anfang at the beginning
die Angst, ⁻e fear
ich habe Angst (vor + *dat*) I am
  afraid *or* frightened (of)
die Anmeldung, -en announcement
die Anstalten (*fpl*) preparations
die Anstrengung, -en effort
die Antwort, -en answer, reply
die Anweisungen (*fpl*) orders,
  instructions
die Anwesenheit presence
das Anzeichen sign, indication
die Anzeige, -n advertisement
der Apparat, -e machine
das Ärgernis, -se annoyance
die Art, -en way, method; kind, sort
auf meine Art in my own way
aller Art of all kinds
der Aufenthalt, -e stay

die Aufmerksamkeit attention;
  attentiveness
die Aufsicht supervision
der Aufstieg, -e ascent
der Ausdruck, ⁻e term, expression
die Auseinandersetzung, -en
  argument
der Ausgangspunkt, -e starting
  point
die Ausnahme, -n exception
die Ausstellung, -en exhibition
die Auswahl, -en (an + *dat*)
  selection (of)
der Bau construction
die Beaufsichtigung supervision
die Bedeutung, -en meaning;
  importance
die Bedingung, -en condition,
  stipulation
das Bedürfnis, -se need
der Befehl, -e order, command
die Begabung, -en talent
der Begriff: im Begriff sein,
  etw zu tun to be about to do sth
das Beispiel, -e example
zum Beispiel for example
die Bemerkung, -en remark
die Bemühung, -en trouble, effort
die Berechnung, -en calculation
der Bescheid, -e message,
  information
  jdm Bescheid sagen to let sb know

sein Bestes tun to do one's best
der Betrag, ⸚e sum, amount
(of money)
der Blödsinn nonsense
die Botschaft, -en message, news;
embassy
die Breite, -n width
der Bursche, -n fellow
die Chance, -n chance, opportunity
der Dank thanks (pl)
die Darstellung, -en portrayal,
representation
das Denken thinking, thought
das Diagramm, -e diagram
die Dicke, -n thickness; fatness
der Dienst, -e service
die Dimension -en dimension
das Ding, -e thing, object
der Duft, ⸚e smell, fragrance
die Dummheit, -en stupidity;
stupid mistake
der Dummkopf, ⸚e idiot
der Dunst, ⸚e vapour
die Ecke, -n corner
die Ehre, -n honour
die Einbildung, -en imagination
der Eindruck, ⸚e impression
der Einfall, ⸚e thought, idea
die Einzelheit, -en detail
die Eleganz elegance
der Empfang, ⸚e reception
die Empfindung, -en feeling,
emotion
das Ende, -n end
zu Ende gehen to end
die Entschlossenheit resolution,
determination
das Ereignis, -se event
die Erfahrung, -en experience

der Erfolg, -e result; success
das Ergebnis, -se result
die Erinnerung, -en memory,
remembrance
die Erklärung, -en explanation
die Erkundigung, -en inquiry
die Erlaubnis, -se permission; permit
das Erlebnis, -se experience
der Ernst seriousness
im Ernst in earnest
das Erstaunen astonishment
die Erwiderung, -en retort
das Exil, -e exile (state)
der Feind, -e enemy
die Flamme, -n flame
die Folge, -n order; series; result
die Form, -en form, shape
die Frage, -n question
Fremde(r), -n, die Fremde, -n
stranger; foreigner
die Freude, -n joy, delight
die Freundlichkeit, -en kindness
die Freundschaft, -en friendship
der Frieden peace
die Frische freshness
der Führer guide; leader
die Gebühr, -en fee, charge
das Gedächtnis, -se memory
der Gedanke, -n thought
die Geduld patience
die Gefahr, -en danger
der Gegenstand, ⸚e object
das Gegenteil, -e opposite
im Gegenteil on the contrary
die Gegenwart present
das Geheimnis, -se mystery; secret
die Gelegenheit, -en opportunity,
occasion
das Gerät, -e device, tool

das Geräusch, -e sound, noise
der Geruch, ¨e smell
das Geschick, -e fate; skill
der Geselle, -n fellow
der Gesichtspunkt, -e point of view
das Glück luck; happiness
der Gott, ¨er god
der (liebe) Gott God
der Grund, ¨e reason
die Gruppe, -n group
die Grüße *(mpl)* wishes
die Güte kindness
die Hauptsache, -n the main thing
der Heimweg, -e way home
die Herstellung, -en manufacture
die Hilfe help
der Hintergrund, ¨e background
die Hoffnung, -en hope
die Höflichkeit, -en politeness
die Höhe, -n height; level
die Idee, -n idea
das Interesse, -n interest
der Kampf, ¨e fight, battle
die Kapelle, -n chapel
das Kapitel chapter
die Katastrophe, -n disaster, catastrophe
die Kenntnis, -se knowledge
der Kerl, -e fellow, chap
die Kette, -n chain
der Klang, ¨e sound
die Klimaanlage air conditioning
der Kollege, -n, die Kollegin colleague
die Konstruktion, -en construction
die Kontrolle, -n control, supervision
die Kopie, -n copy

der Korb, ¨e basket
die Kosten *(pl)* cost(s); expenses
der Kreis, -e circle; district
der Krieg, -e war
der Kurort, -e health resort
der Kuss, ¨e kiss
das Lächeln smile
die Lage, -n situation
die Länge, -n length
die Lang(e)weile boredom
der Lärm noise
der Laut, -e sound
das Leben life
der Lebenslauf, ¨e CV
das Leid sorrow, grief
der Leiter chief, leader
der Leser, die Leserin reader
das Licht, -er light
die Liebe, -n love
die Linie, -n line
die Liste, -n list
die Literatur literature
das Loch, ¨er hole
die Lösung, -en solution
die Lücke, -n opening, gap
die Lüge, -n lie
die Lust: ich habe Lust, es zu tun I feel like doing it
die Macht, ¨e power
das Magazin, -e magazine
der Mangel, ¨e (an + *dat*) lack (of), shortage (of)
die Maschine, -n machine
das Maximum, -a maximum
die Meinung, -en opinion, view
meiner Meinung nach in my opinion
das meiste; die meisten most
die Meldung, -en announcement

die Menge, -n crowd; quantity, lot
das Minimum, -a minimum
die Mischung, -en mixture
das Missgeschick, -e misfortune
das Mitleid sympathy
die Mitteilung, -en communication
das Mittel means; method
das Modell, -e model, version
die Möglichkeit, -en means; possibility
sein Möglichstes tun to do one's best
die Mühe, -n pains, trouble
die Münze, -n coin
der Mut courage, spirit
die Nachrichten (fpl) news; information
der Nachteil, -e disadvantage
die Nähe: in der Nähe close by
das Netz, -e network
die Not need, distress
die Notiz, -en note, item
die Nummer, -n number
das Objekt, -e object
die Öffentlichkeit the general public
die Öffnung, -en opening
die Ordnung, -en order
in Ordnung bringen to arrange, tidy (up)
alles ist in Ordnung everything is all right
der Ort, -e place
das Pech misfortune, bad luck
der Pfeil, -e arrow
das Pfund, -e pound (sterling); pound (weight)
der Plan, ⁻e plan; map

der Platz, ⁻e place; seat; room, space; square
die Politik politics; policy
das Porträt, -s portrait
das Problem, -e problem
das Produkt, -e product; produce
der Punkt, -e point; dot; full stop
die Puppe, -n doll
die Qualität, -en quality
der Radau hullaballoo
der Rand, ⁻er edge; rim
der Rat, -schläge (piece of) advice
das Rätsel puzzle, riddle
der Rauch smoke
der Raum, Räume space; room
das Recht, -e law; justice; right
recht haben to be right
die Rede, -n speech
eine Rede halten to make a speech
die Regierung, -en government; reign
die Reihe, -n series; line
ich bin an der Reihe it's my turn now
der Reiz, -e attraction, charm
die Reklame, -n advertisement
der Rest remainder, rest
die Reste (mpl) remains
das Resultat, -e result
der Revolutionär, -e revolutionary
der Rhythmus, -men rhythm
die Richtung, -en direction
die Rückseite, -n back (of page etc)
der Ruf, -e call, cry; reputation
die Ruhe rest; peace; calm; silence
die Sache, -n thing; matter
der Schein, -e (bank) note
ein 20-Euro-Schein a 20-euro note
das Schicksal, -e fate
das Schild, -er sign; label

der Schlag, ⁝e blow, knock
der Schluss, ⁝e end(ing)
am Schluss at the end
der Schmutz, die Schmutzigkeit
  dirt, dirtiness
der Schrei, -e cry, scream
der Schritt, -e footstep; step, pace
die Schuld fault
ich bin nicht schuld daran it's not
  my fault
die Schwierigkeit, -en difficulty
die Sensation, -en stir, sensation
die Serie, -n series
die Sicherheit, -en security; safety
die Sicht sight; view
der Sieg, -e victory
der Sinn, -e mind; sense; meaning
die Situation, -en situation
die Sorge, -n care, worry
sich (dat) Sorgen machen to be
  worried
die Sorte, -n sort, kind
das Souvenir, -s souvenir
der Spalt crack, opening; split
die Spalte, -n column (of page)
der Spaß, ⁝e fun; joke
der Spektakel hullaballo
das Spielzeug, -e toy
die Spur, -en sign, trace
der Staat, -en state
der Standpunkt, -e point of view,
  standpoint
die Stärke, -n power, strength
die Stelle, -n place
die Steuer, -n tax
der Stil, -e style
die Stille quietness
die Stimmung, -en mood;
  atmosphere

die Strecke, -n stretch; distance
das Stück, -e piece, part
die Summe, -n sum
das System, -e system
das Talent, -e talent
in der Tat in (actual) fact, indeed
die Tätigkeit, -en activity
der Teil, -e, das Teil, -e part, section
der Text, -e text
der Titel title
die Tiefe, -n depth
der Traum, ⁝e dream
der Treffpunkt, -e meeting place
der Trost comfort
die Trümmer (pl) wreckage; ruins
der Typ, -en type
Überlebende(r), -n survivor
die Überraschung, -en surprise
die Umgebung, -en surroundings
  (pl)
das Unglück, -e misfortune;
  bad luck; disaster
das Unheil evil; disaster,
  misfortune
das Unrecht: unrecht haben to be
  wrong, be mistaken
die Unterbrechung, -en
  interruption
die Unterhaltung, -en
  conversation, chat
das Unternehmen undertaking,
  enterprise
der Unterschied, -e difference
der Urlaub, -e holidays,leave
die Ursache, -n reason, cause
die Verabredung, -en appointment
die Verbindung, -en connection
der Vergleich, -e comparison
das Vergnügen pleasure

der Versuch, -e attempt
das Vertrauen confidence
die Vorbereitung, -en preparation
der Vorschlag, -̈e suggestion
die Vorsicht care, caution
die Vorstellung, -en introduction; idea, thought
der Vorteil, -e advantage
die Wahl, -en choice, selection; election
der Wähler voter
die Wahrheit, -en truth
der Wechselkurs, -e exchange rate
die Weile, -n while
die Weise, -n way, method, manner
auf diese Weise in this way or manner
die Weite, -n width; distance
die Werbung, -en advertising
der Wert, -e value
die Wette, -n bet

die Wichtigkeit importance
die Wirklichkeit, -en fact, reality
die Wirkung, -en effect
der Witz, -e joke
der Wohlstand prosperity
das Wort, -̈er or -e word
der Wunsch, -̈e wish
die Wut rage, fury
die Zahl, -en number, figure
das Zeichen sign
die Zeile, -n line (of text)
die Zeitschrift, -en magazine
die Zeitung, -en newspaper
das Zentrum, Zentren centre
das Zeug stuff; gear
das Ziel, -e aim, goal; destination
das Ziffer, -n number, figure
der Zorn anger
die Zutaten (pl) ingredients
der Zweck, -e purpose

PREPOSITIONS AND CONJUNCTIONS

What is a preposition?

A preposition is one word such as *at, for, with, into* or *from*, or words such as *in front of* or *near to*, which are usually followed by a noun or a pronoun or, in English, a word ending in *-ing*.

Prepositions show how people and things relate to the rest of the sentence, for example, *She's at home; It's for you; You'll get into trouble; It's in front of you.*

What is a conjunction?

A conjunction is a word such as *and, but, or, so, if* and *because*, that links two words or phrases of a similar type, or two parts of a sentence, for example, *Diane and I have been friends for years; I left because I was bored.*

aber but; however
als when; as; than
als ob, als wenn as if, as though
also therefore, so
anstatt (+ *gen*) instead of
außer (+ *dat*) out of; except
außerhalb (+ *gen*) outside
bei (+ *dat*) near, by; at the house of
bevor before (*time*)
bis until, till (*conj*); (+ *acc*) until; (up) to, as far as
da as, since, seeing (that)
damit so that, in order that
dass that
denn for
ehe before
entweder ... oder either... or
gegenüber (+ *dat*) opposite; to(wards)
gerade als just as
hinter (+ *dat or acc*) behind
indem es, while
innerhalb (+ *gen*) in(side), within

je ..., desto the more ... the more
nachdem after
nun (da) now (that)
ob if, whether
obwohl although
oder or
ohne dass without
seit (+ *dat*) since
sobald as soon as
sodass so that
solange as long as
sondern (*after neg*) but
nicht nur ... sondern auch not only ... but also
sowohl ... als (auch) both... and
statt (+ *gen*) instead of
stattdessen instead
teils ... teils partly ... partly
trotz (+ *gen*) despite, in spite of
und and
während while (*conj*); (+ *gen*) during (*prep*)
weder ... noch neither ... nor

wegen (+ *gen*) because of
weil because
wenn when; if

wenn ... auch although; even if
wie as, like

VERBS

> **What is a verb?**
> A **verb** is a 'doing' word which describes what somebody or something does, what they are, or what happens to them, for example, *play*, *be*, *disappear*.

abhängen von to depend on
abholen to fetch, go and meet (*somebody*)
ablehnen to refuse
abnehmen to lose weight
abschreiben to copy
akzeptieren to accept
anbeten to adore
anbieten to give, offer
anblicken to look (at)
ändern: seine Meinung ändern to change one's mind
anfangen to begin
angeben to state
angehören (*+ dat*) to belong to (*club etc*)
angreifen to attack; to touch
anhalten to stop; to continue
ankommen to arrive
ankündigen to announce
annehmen to accept; to assume
anschalten to switch on
antworten to answer, reply
anzeigen to announce
anziehen to attract; to put (on) (*clothes*)
sich ärgern to get angry
atmen to breathe
aufbewahren to keep, store
aufhängen to hang (up)
aufheben to raise, lift

aufhören to stop
aufkleben to stick on *or* onto
aufmachen to open
aufpassen (auf + *acc*) to watch; to be careful (of)
aufstehen to get up
aufwachen to wake up (*intransitive*)
aufwärmen to warm (up)
aufwecken to awaken, wake up (*transitive*)
ausdrücken to express
ausführen to carry out, execute
ausgeben to spend (*money*)
ausleihen to borrow
auslöschen to put out, extinguish
ausrufen to exclaim, cry (out)
sich ausruhen to rest
ausschalten to switch off
ausschlafen to have a good sleep
aussprechen to pronounce
ausstrecken to extend, hold out
sich ausstrecken to stretch out
auswählen to select
beabsichtigen to intend
beachten to observe, obey
sich (bei jdm) bedanken to say thank you (to sb)
bedauern to regret
bedecken to cover
bedeuten to mean
bedienen to serve; to operate

sich beeilen to hurry
beenden to finish
befehlen (+ dat) to order
sich befinden to be
begegnen (+ dat) to meet
beginnen to begin
begreifen to realize
behalten to keep, retain
behaupten to maintain
beherrschen to rule (over)
sich beklagen (über + acc) to
 complain (about)
bekommen to obtain
bemerken to notice
benachrichtigen to inform
benutzen to use
beobachten to watch
berichten to report
(sich) beruhigen to calm down
sich beschäftigen mit to attend to;
 to be concerned with
beschmutzen to dirty
beschreiben to describe
(be)schützen (vor + dat) to protect
 (from)
sich beschweren (über + acc)
 to complain (about)
besiegen to conquer
besitzen to own, possess
besprechen to discuss
bestehen (aus + dat) to consist (of),
 comprise
bestehen (auf + dat) to insist
 (upon)
bestellen to order
besuchen to attend, be present at,
 go to, visit
betreten to enter
beunruhigen to worry

(sich) bewegen to move
bewundern to admire
biegen to bend
bieten to offer
binden to tie
bitten to request
bitten um to ask for
bleiben to stay, remain
blicken (auf + acc) to glance (at),
 look (at)
borgen to borrow;
 jdm etw borgen to lend sb sth
brauchen to need
brechen to break
brennen to burn
bringen to bring, take
bummeln to wander; to skive
danken (+ dat) to thank
darstellen to represent
dauern to last
decken to cover
denken to think, believe
denken an (+ acc) to think of;
 to remember
denken über (+ acc) to think about;
 to reflect on
deuten (auf + acc) to point (to or at)
dienen to serve
diskutieren to discuss
drehen to turn; to shoot (film)
drucken to print
drücken to press, squeeze
durchführen to accomplish, carry
 out
durchqueren to cross, pass
 through
durchsuchen to search
dürfen to be allowed to
eilen to rush, dash

einfallen (+ *dat*) to occur
  (*to someone*)
einladen to invite
einrichten to establish, set up
einschalten to switch on
einschlafen to fall asleep
eintreten to come in
einwickeln to wrap (up)
empfangen to receive (*person*)
empfehlen to recommend
entdecken to discover
entführen to take away
enthalten to contain
(sich) entscheiden to decide
sich entschließen to make up one's
  mind
entschuldigen to excuse
sich entschuldigen (für) to
  apologize (for)
enttäuschen to disappoint
(sich) entwickeln to develop
sich ereignen to happen
erfahren to learn; to experience;
  erfahren von to hear about
erfolgreich successful
ergreifen to seize
erhalten to receive, get
sich erheben to rise
erinnern (an + *acc*) to remind (of)
sich erinnern (an + *acc*) to
  remember
erkennen to recognize
erklären to state; to explain
sich erkundigen (nach *or* **über** +
  acc) to inquire about
erlauben to allow, permit, let
erleben to experience
ermutigen to encourage
erobern to capture

erregen to disturb, excite
erreichen to reach; to catch
  (*train etc*)
errichten to erect
erschaffen to create
erscheinen to appear
erschrecken to frighten
erschüttern to shake, rock, stagger
erstaunen to astonish
erwachen to wake up (*intransitive*)
erwähnen to mention
erwarten to expect, await, wait for
erwidern to retort
erzählen to tell, explain
erziehen to bring up, educate
fallen to fall
fallen lassen to drop
falten to fold
fangen to catch
fassen to grasp; to comprehend
fehlen to be missing;
er fehlt mir I miss him
etw fertig machen to bring sth
  about; to get sth ready
festbinden to tie, fasten
finden to find
fliehen (vor + *dat*, **aus)** to flee
  (from)
fließen (in + *acc*) to flow (into)
flüstern to whisper
folgen (+ *dat*) to follow
fordern to demand
fortgehen to go away
fortfahren to depart; to continue
fortsetzen to continue (*transitive*)
fragen to ask
sich fragen to wonder
sich freuen to be glad
führen to lead

füllen to fill
funkeln to sparkle
funktionieren to work (*of machine*)
sich fürchten (vor + *dat*) to
  be afraid *or* frightened (of)
geben to give
gebrauchen to use
gefallen (+ *dat*) to please;
  das gefällt mir I like that
gehen to go
gehorchen (+ *dat*) to obey
gehören (+ *dat*) to belong (to)
gelingen (+ *dat*) to succeed
gelten to be worth
genießen to enjoy
genügen to be sufficient
gern haben to like
geschehen to happen
gestatten to permit, allow
glauben (+ *dat*) to believe
glauben an (+ *acc*) to believe in
glühen to glow
gründen to establish
gucken to look
haben to have
halten to keep; to stop; to hold
  sich irren to be mistaken
halten für to consider (as)
handeln: es handelt sich um it is
  a question of
hängen to hang (up)
hassen to hate, loathe
hauen to cut, hew
heben to lift, raise
heimbringen to take home
helfen (+ *dat*) to help
herantreten an (+ *acc*) to approach
herausziehen to pull out
hereinkommen to enter, come in

hereinlassen to admit
herstellen to produce,
  manufacture
herunterlassen to lower
hineingehen (in + *acc*) to enter,
  go in (to)
hinlegen to put down
sich hinsetzen to sit down
hinstellen to put down
hinübergehen to go through;
  to go over
hinweisen to point out
hinweisen auf (+ *acc*) to refer.to
hinzufügen to add
hoffen (auf + *acc*) to hope (for)
holen to fetch
horchen to listen
hören to hear
hüten to guard, watch over
interessieren to interest
sich für etw interessieren to be
  interested in sth
kämpfen to fight
kennen to know (*person, place*)
kennenlernen to meet, get to
  know
klagen to complain
klatschen to gossip
klettern to climb
klingeln to ring
klingen to sound
kochen to cook
kommen to come
können to be able (to)
kriegen to get, obtain
sich kümmern (um) to worry
  (about)
küssen to kiss
lassen to allow, let; to leave

laufen to run
leben to live
legen to lay
sich legen to lie down
leid tun (+ dat) to feel sorry for
du tust mir leid I feel sorry for you
es tut mir leid I'm sorry
leiden to suffer; **ich kann ihn nicht leiden** I can't stand him
leihen to lend; **sich** (dat) **etw leihen** to borrow sth
leiten to guide, lead
lesen to read
lieben to love
liefern to deliver; to supply
liegen to be (situated)
loben to praise
löschen to put out
lösen to buy (ticket)
losmachen to unfasten undo, untie
loswerden to get rid of
lügen to lie, tell a lie
machen to do; to make
malen to paint
meinen to think, believe
mieten to hire, rent
mitbringen to bring
mitnehmen to take
mitteilen: jdm etw mitteilen to inform sb of sth
mögen to like
murmeln to murmur
müssen to have to (must), be obliged to
nachdenken (über + acc) to think (about)
nachsehen to check
nähen to sew

sich nähern (+ dat) to approach
nehmen to take
nennen to call, name
sich niederlegen to go to bed, lie down
notieren to note
öffnen to open
organisieren to organize
passen (+ dat) to suit, be suitable
passieren to happen
pflegen to take care of
plaudern to chat
pressen to press, squeeze
produzieren to produce
programmieren to program
protestieren to protest
prüfen to examine, check
rasieren to shave
raten (+ dat) to advise
räumen to clear away
reden to talk, speak
reinigen to clean, tidy up
reisen to go, travel
retten to save, rescue
riechen (nach) to smell (of)
rufen to call
sich rühren to stir
sagen (+ dat) to say (to), tell
säubern to clean
saugen to suck
schaden (+ dat) to harm
schallen to sound
schauen (auf + acc) to look (at)
scheinen to seem; to shine
schieben to push, shove
schießen to shoot
schlafen to sleep
schlafen gehen to go to bed
schlagen to hit, strike, knock, beat

supplementary vocabulary

sich schlagen to fight
(sich) schließen to close, shut
schneiden to cut
schnüren to tie
schreiben to write
schreien to shout, cry
schütteln to shake
schützen (vor + dat) to protect
 (from)
schweigen to be silent
schwören to swear
sehen to see
sein to be
senken to lower
setzen to put (down), place, set
sich setzen to settle, sit (down)
seufzen to sigh
singen to sing
sitzen to sit, be sitting
sollen ought (to)
sorgen für to take care of, look after
sich sorgen (um) to worry (about)
sparen to save
spaßen to joke
spazieren gehen to go for a walk
sprechen to speak
stattfinden to take place
stecken to put, stick
stehen to stand
stehen bleiben to stop (still)
steigen to come or go up, rise;
 to climb
stellen to put, place; to ask
 (a question)
sterben to die
stimmen to be right
stoppen to stop (transitive)
stören to disturb
stoßen to push, shove

strecken to stretch
streiten to argue, fight
sich streiten to quarrel
stürzen to fall, crash
sich stürzen (in or auf + acc) to rush
 or dash (into)
suchen to look for, search for
tanzen to dance
teilen to share, divide
teilnehmen (an + dat) to attend,
 be present at, go to, take part (in)
töten to kill
tragen to carry; to wear
träumen to dream
treffen to meet; to strike (transitive)
trennen to separate; to divide
treiben to drive; to go in for
trocknen to dry
tun to do
so tun, als ob to pretend (that)
überlegen to consider, reflect
überraschen to surprise
überreden to persuade
übersetzen to translate
(sich) umdrehen to turn round
umgeben sein von to be
 surrounded with or by
umgehen to avoid, bypass
umkehren to turn
umleiten to divert
umwerfen to overturn, knock over
unterbrechen to interrupt
unterhalten to support
(sich) unterhalten (über + acc)
 to converse or talk (about);
 to entertain
sich unterscheiden to differ,
 be different
unterschreiben to sign

untersuchen to examine
sich verabreden to make an
  appointment
verbessern to improve
verbieten to forbid, prohibit
verbinden to connect; to bandage
verbringen to pass or spend (time)
verdecken to hide, cover up
verderben to spoil, ruin
verdienen to deserve
vereinigen to unite
vergessen to forget
sich verhalten to act, behave
verhindern to prevent
verlangen to demand, order
verlassen to leave
verleihen (an + acc) to lend (to)
verletzen to harm
verlieren to lose
es vermeiden, etw zu tun to avoid
  doing sth
vermieten to let, rent
versäumen to miss
(ver)schließen to lock
verschwinden to disappear, vanish
versehen (mit) to provide
versichern (+ dat) to convince,
  assure
versprechen to promise
(sich) verstecken (vor + dat) to hide
  (from)
verstehen to understand;
  was verstehen Sie darunter?
  what do you understand by that?
versuchen to try, taste, sample;
  to attempt to
verteidigen to defend
verteilen to distribute
verzeihen to pardon, forgive

vollenden to finish
vorbereiten to prepare
vorgeben to pretend
vorschlagen to suggest
(sich) vorstellen to introduce
  (oneself)
sich (dat) etw vorstellen to
  imagine sth
wachen to be awake
wachsen to grow
wagen to dare
wählen to elect; to choose
warten (auf + acc) to wait (for)
(sich) waschen to wash
wechseln to exchange; to change
  (money)
wecken to awaken, wake up
  (transitive)
wegnehmen to take off or away
sich weigern to refuse
weinen to cry
sich wenden an (+ acc) to apply to;
  to turn (to)
werden to become, grow, turn (out)
werfen to throw
wetten (auf + acc) to bet (on)
wiederholen to repeat
wiedersehen to see again
wischen to wipe
wissen to know
wohnen (in + dat) to live (in)
wohnen (bei + dat) to lodge (with),
  live (with)
wollen to want (to), wish (to)
sich wundern (über + acc)
  to wonder (at), be astonished
  (at or by)
es wundert mich I am surprised
  (at it)

das würde mich wundern!
 that would surprise me!
wünschen to wish
zählen to count
zeichnen to draw
zeigen to show, point
zelten to go camping
zerbrechen to break
zerreißen to tear up
zerstören to demolish, destroy
zerstreuen to scatter
ziehen to draw; to pull; to tug

zittern (vor + *dat***)** to tremble (with)
zögern to hesitate
zugeben to confess, admit
zuhören (+ *dat*) to listen (to)
zumachen to close, shut (*transitive*)
zunehmen to put on weight
zurückkehren to come back, return
zurückkommen to go *or* come back
zurücksetzen, zurückstellen to
 replace
zweifeln to doubt
zwingen to force, oblige

ENGLISH
INDEX

The words on the following pages cover all of the
ESSENTIAL and IMPORTANT NOUNS in the book.